THE ALCHEMY OF VOICE

Transform and Enrich Your Life
Through the Power of Your Voice

FINDHORN PRESS

Also by Stewart Pearce

BOOK

The Heart's Note

SET OF CARDS

Angels of Atlantis Oracle Cards

CDS/MP3S

The Alchemy of Voice - Awakening
The Alchemy of Voice - Initiation
Sonic Meditations

BOOK, SET OF CARDS AND MP3S
AVAILABLE FROM
www.findhornpress.com

CDS AVAILABLE FROM
www.thealchemyofvoice.com

THE ALCHEMY OF VOICE

Transform and Enrich Your Life
Through the Power of Your Voice

STEWART PEARCE

 FINDHORN PRESS

First published in Great Britain in 2005 by Hodder and Stoughton
This revised second edition published in 2010 by Findhorn Press

ISBN 978-1-84409-194-2

A CIP record for this title is available from the British Library.

Edited by Nicky Leach
Front cover design by Richard Crookes
Interior by Damian Keenan
Printed and bound in the European Union

Published by

Findhorn Press

117-121 High Street,

Forres IV36 1AB,

Scotland, UK

t +44 (0)1309 690582

f +44 (0)131 777 2711

e info@findhornpress.com

www.findhornpress.com

ACKNOWLEDGMENTS

I send gratitude to all my sources of inspiration: the students, actors, directors, teachers, clients, guides, and of course the Angels—without whom none of this material would exist. This information has flowed as a result of the passionate, evocative, stirringly creative, energetic exchanges we have had over many years.

A passionate thank you to Thierry Bogliolo at Findhorn Press, who believed in the pioneering fervor of '*The Alchemy of Voice*' and who encouraged and supported the re-formation of the original manuscript to include a greater revelation of the work and its origin.

Thanks must also go to my literary agent Kay McCauley, whose heart-felt conviction and stalwart support has been truly remarkable.

In conclusion, much love and thanks to Mark Rylance, who once pioneered the vision of a brightly lit beacon in the form of Shakespeare's Globe, giving life to the beautiful words of William Shakespeare, and whose contribution to my life and work has been immeasurable. Mark is not only one of the most gifted Actors of this time, but also gives embodiment to the notion of the Human Angel, without whom life would be a desert of prosaic inevitability.

Stewart Pearce,
March 2010

Contents

Foreword

Man know thyself and thou shalt know the Universe

These words appeared above the pillars of Hercules, the entry point to the temples of the ancient Greek mystery schools, and perhaps are a fitting tribute to the entry point of this text.

Stewart Pearce is the Master of Voice at Shakespeare's Globe Theatre. He works with the actors to aid us all to meet the wonderful opportunity of speaking in an amphitheater built for sound; an amphitheater built also for some of the most beautiful sounds conjured by the English language, under the feather of William Shakespeare.

When we gather the actors on the first day of rehearsal at the Globe, I particularly love the pregnant moment of silence before I start to impart welcomes, introductions, and all the information that enables a group of skilled craftspeople to make something as elusive as a production of a Shakespeare play. I try to woo this expectant moment of stillness before business by reading a poem, and this year I read this:

This we have now
Is not imagination

This is not grief or joy

Not a judging state
Or an elation
Or sadness

These come
And go
This is the presence
That doesn't
It's dawn, Husam
Here in the splendor of coral

Inside the friend, the simple truth
Of what Hallaj said

What else could human beings want?

When grapes turn to wine
They're wanting
This

When the nightsky pours by
It's really a crowd of beggars
And they all want some of this!

This
That we are now
Created the body, cell by cell
Like bees building a honeycomb

The Human body and the Universe
Grew from this,
Not this
From the Universe and the Human body

—*RUMI*

(TRANSLATION BY COLEMAN BARKS
AND JOHN MOYNE)

Rumi writes of presence, and when I dare to read aloud one of his resonant thoughts I draw on all of my work with Stewart. To speak thoughts like these above requires the *sound* of a certain easy presence and honesty. How does one develop such a voice?

The Mayan culture has a belief that has been told to me as this. The world is created by song, which is sung continually by the gods. Everything we receive via our senses is a manifestation of the vibrations of this song, sung on the etheric plane of existence. In a way, this belief is not far from the scientific belief that all matter is just vibrating energy.

The Mayans also teach us that the laws of courtesy apply on the etheric plane as much as among human beings. Greetings, farewells, gifts, praise, acknowledgment and, primarily, thanks for creation are very helpful. The Mayan gods appreciate beauty in the way we appreciate food; it feeds them. Beautiful sounds are particularly loved and can be witnessed in the incredible sound of the indigenous people's language. Their prayers, as I have heard them, are full of descriptions of the natural world, expressed in a wild poetry of image and love. Only Shakespeare comes close to this in our culture.

Singing or speaking beautifully to the Mayan gods increases their ability to sing the world into creation. A kind of song cycle is set up that empowers everything. A similar phenomenon is easily witnessed when humans listen to a beautiful speaker or singer.

There was a time that a father would listen to a young man who came to woo his daughter. He wouldn't be fooled by the way the man looked, but would welcome him by how well spoken he was. Honesty, wit, self-knowledge, suffering, soul, faithfulness, and the general connectedness of a person can all be heard in a person's voice. It is their persona.

And it was Confucius who stated that one changes society by first changing society's language.

Stewart has helped me—as an actor and a person—to meet these challenging ideas without fear. He does not impose a voice but works to release the sound that is true to the individual, to you. He has given my sound the earth or ground to stand upon. On occasion, the sounds he has helped me make have stirred a deep place within, memories or fears of who I am. It seems that the increased consciousness of myself, particularly those parts in shadow, is an aspect of the resonance I seek as a speaker. Stewart's instinctive and practiced understanding and knowledge of the vibrations of sound—the effect that the actual sound makes on a speaker and listener, never mind the thought and emotion—is a rare gift.

His gift has saved me—an artistic director and actor—thousands of pounds. In the early years of the reconstructed Shakespeare's Globe Theatre I was about to spend thousands of pounds on "acoustic baffling" because I and my fellow actors were having difficulty being heard—then I met Stewart.

If he has managed to express even a tenth of that gift in his writing of this book, this will be an inspiration and a great gift to all who read it.

MARK RYLANCE
Actor & Artistic Director of Shakespeare's Globe Theater
May 2004

Introduction

The human voice is a wondrous thing. From the first roar of life, as we take our first breath, we use our voices to connect with the world. The sounds we make, the tones we use, the words we choose, all direct and shape our identity. We buy a cappuccino, swear undying love, declare war, praise from our hearts, damn, correct, and reject, all by breathing and opening our mouths to create sound.

The voice can move us to tears, shatter a glass, or heal a broken heart. It can mesmerize, seduce, infuriate, or command—inspire fear and dread, trust and love. The sound of a voice can evoke memories, sensations, thoughts, and feelings. It has an awesome force to make or break strong bonds, to torture or uplift, create or destroy. The voice, therefore, lies at the core of our personal power and resonates the essence of our truth.

Voices affect us not only with their words but with the many other sounds we noisy creatures make. Think of how infectious and joyful laughter can be. Think of soaring musical notes and how they can transport us into glorious scenarios. Think of groans of pain, sobs of despair, and the profoundly unhappy effect they can have on us.

Such is the power of the voice. Yet many of us take our own voice completely for granted. We use it as an everyday tool, seldom giving it a second thought. We may like it, or we may feel it's too high, low, loud, or quiet, but most of the time we simply use it without thinking.

The voice is a glorious gift. It carries the potential for great influence, over ourselves as well as others. Used to its full capacity, your voice has the power to affect your life in a multitude of wonderful ways, and when you begin to understand and work with it, it becomes far more than something that simply trips from the end of your tongue. When it is connected to your heart and comes from deep within you, then it will have the power to transform your life. When you speak with your true voice, which means using your own unique "signature note," you will feel and live with true authenticity. Your confidence levels will soar, and that sense of self—of being someone who is both heard and who hears others—will be greatly increased. As a result your ability to achieve what you want in life will be powerfully and vitally enhanced.

What you want may be practical, emotional, or spiritual. It may be a new job or career, a higher profile, deeper self-knowledge, illuminating self-confidence, the ability to give talks and presentations with ease, to heal a wound from the past, or simply to learn to speak with ease and fluency. It may be a transformation for your body and feelings, a wish to communicate more deeply, or a deeper sense of being balanced in mind, body, and spirit. Whatever it is, you can use your voice to achieve a new state of being. Literally, any challenge will be a thing of the past!

Your voice is your identity in sound. It tells the world, through its position, tone, resonance, energy, and expression, who you are. Most of us use an "everyday" voice that we have adapted to fit social expectations or what we feel is our role in life. This "everyday" voice is often very different from our truly authentic voice.

In the West we live in a world that is largely intellectualized. We are taught from a very young age to believe that thinking is the only thing that counts, while feelings remain suppressed. We are taught to hold back, to be reserved and silent, to analyze rather than express, and to refrain from speaking our thoughts and feelings. The result is that we diminish and restrain one of our most glorious assets—the voice of our true self.

The nature of our true voice can only be discovered by recognizing and allowing our true feelings to be expressed. When we cease to suppress our feelings, we cease to hold back our true voice. We can speak out clearly, with resonance, from the depth of our soul, as our one and only voice is the sound of our truth and, therefore, a means for revelation.

I fundamentally believe that we have "forgotten" or "un-remembered" the very core of our sound and have moved away from the passion of feeling that gives this core sound its magnificent quality. My aim is to help you rediscover your true voice and to express it with energy and joy, dispelling fear from your heart, mind, and soul and illuminating all your communication processes.

About Me

As far back as I can remember I have been enchanted by the sound of the human voice. When I heard voices as a very young child I saw the sound as color around me. If someone was angry, a violent red would streak toward me; a whining, complaining voice would appear as dark yellow; while my mother's soothing and comforting humming bathed me in a pure white light.

I didn't speak until I was five and couldn't read until I was ten. No matter how hard I worked, I simply couldn't make sense of the written word. It was only the sounds I heard and the colors I saw that made sense. It must have been around the age of seven that I recollect becoming consciously aware of the power of the word not only as a color but as a sound shape that conveyed rich meaning. Fortunately, both my parents were great storytellers, and I loved to listen to their escapades.

My father worked for the royal household and would tell tales of his travels with Prince Philip to exotic lands: the beauty of Machu Picchu or tiger shoots in India. My mother read copious stories to me, while I would listen in delight, feeling the currents of energy from the stories running through me and around me. Mother brought the power of her heart through her voice and the power of her soul through the desire of her intention. This was her gift to me; through her voice, she revealed wisdom and knowledge.

When I was ten it was decided that I would join a church choir, and through this I discovered the beauty of sacred song and, miraculously, the ability to read. As I felt the force of exquisite music such as Handel's *Messiah* move through me, I found myself able to connect the energy of sound with the word; in short, the sound connected me with the printed notes that eventually became the printed words lying beneath. Much later I learned that I had a condition known as synesthesia, a sensory crossover through which something is perceived by one sense and transformed by another; hence, the ability to see sound as a color.

Moving to secondary school allowed me to discover the two great passions of my life: theater and ritual. These forces were suspended in my imagination as a result of growing up within the atmosphere of Buckingham Palace; the rituals of protocol, manners, and form were essential attributes of royal life, and for me the ritual and theater of state occasions were magnificent. At school I began taking part in plays, which I loved, and as I attended a Church of England Anglo-Catholic school, I also took part in the ritual liturgy of Mass. Home was near St James's Palace, a stone's throw from London's West End, and my parents were keen theatergoers, often taking me to shows. On one such visit, when I was very young, I asked my mother where we were. She answered, "We are in a place of magic." I was captured and enraptured.

I loved acting in school plays and was told that my voice had a healing or soothing quality. I became determined to find a way of telling stories professionally through ritual, whether as an actor or a priest. After leaving school I trained as an actor-teacher through an interest in theater in education. I went on to work as a peripatetic speech and drama teacher, after which I worked as an actor in some of the burgeoning repertory theaters that existed in the United Kingdom. My work as an actor also took me to the United States.

It was at this time that I met and worked with Cicely Berry, Voice Director of the Royal Shakespeare Company. Observing Ciss coach actors brought me back to the magic of my beliefs. Under her guidance, an actor could find a physically rooted connection between breath and thought, and consequently, the voice would become the pure conductor of intention, resulting in the listener becoming entranced or "magnetized" by the sound.

It was Cicely who gave me my first job in 1980, as a voice coach at the Guildhall School of Music and Drama. From there I moved to the Webber Douglas Academy of Dramatic Art, where I was Head of Voice for seventeen years. For me, Webber Douglas became a laboratory in which I was able to develop and shape my craft. While I was there, I explored the notion that we each have our own "signature note": an elemental sound that is often given away with our personal power in fearful or conflicting situations. Once we reconnect with our voice's physical power, we can create a magnificent harmony among our physical, emotional, mental, and spiritual bodies. At this time, I also reconnected with and developed a knowledge of how the chakras—the body's energy centers, which are placed at seven points along the spine—can be rebalanced through the voice, charging the body with healing and bringing back an astonishing sense of wholeness.

What developed from these experiences was a private practice and opportunities to teach master classes internationally—in Canada, Australia, Belgium, France, Spain, Denmark, and throughout the United States.

In 1998, Mark Rylance invited me to become Resident Master of Voice at the rebuilt Shakespeare's Globe Theatre in London. This opened up many other opportunities, such as work at the Chicago Shakespeare Theater. At this time I became the Head of Voice at the Drama Center London and also helped to create a Conservatory at Shakespeare's Globe for the classical training of young American actors.

I have always worked to extend knowledge of the power of the voice beyond the entertainment industry, and have consulted in many other industries for more than ten years, working as a presentation consultant for companies such as L'Oréal, Merrill Lynch, British Telecom, and ITN.

The Alchemy of Voice is my opportunity to pass on to an even wider audience all that I have learned about the extraordinary, unique, and exciting power of the human voice.

What this book holds for you

The knowledge contained within this book will help every reader to step onto the path of happiness. Our voice is a means for revelation; if we are aware that we can harmonize ourselves through its power, we can move from negative disenchantment to knowing what is enchanting about our lives. I will introduce you to the awesome power of sound and the ability of the human voice to bring about transformation and balance. I want you to discover the magnificent power you have within you and how this can be simply expressed through your voice. Knowing how to use it to your best advantage in every area of your life will open doors and bring you joy and success.

I will show you how to reconnect with the *anima,* or life force, that exists within the universe and in each one of us, so that with the power of your voice you can transform or transmute yourself from a negative to a positive state of being. I will show you how your voice is at the very core of your humanity and how to speak or sound the "song of your soul"—a means by which you may convey the essence of who you are. I will take you on a journey of self-discovery and enlightenment that will help you find your "natural" rather than your "normal" voice.

Using straightforward exercises, I will guide you to develop your own signature note. This note is the key to your individuality and self-expression; its expansion will create a sense of joy and confidence in yourself and your abilities. I will show you how you can use your voice to express yourself clearly, to heal your emotional hurts and ill health, and to connect more deeply with others. When this happens you will be seen for who you truly are.

This book encapsulates the *zeitgeist*, or spirit of the times that we are living in. It heralds a new way of relating, in which we will balance the fundamental masculine and feminine elements of our being, using ways of thinking and feeling that come from within, rather than from our surroundings.

In recent times, we in the Western world have become fixated with achieving through "doing" and have abandoned the paramount truth that comes with simply "being." Today, there are signs all around us that this is changing, and we are surrounded by potent guidelines showing us the way forward. This book is one such guideline. It offers a path to harmony and happiness and asks for our voice to be restored in this time of transformation. If we can use our voice as a conduit between the intellect (head) and our feelings (heart) we may reap the profound benefits of this era.

I hope you will travel with me, and that by the journey's end you will feel both enriched and empowered.

CHAPTER 1

The Origin of Sound

He who knows the secret of sound,
knows the mystery of the whole universe.
—*HAZRAT INAYAT KHAN*

Sound has an immense creative force. It is a prime component of molecular energy, affects matter and, therefore, has a dramatic impact on the landscape of the world within and without us. Indeed, from time immemorial it has been believed that sound is at the core of creation and shapes the universe within which we live. Dwell for a moment on the very truth of your birth—in a sense your first creative act. As you entered the world, your first independent action was to breathe, and then to make sound—the sound of your creation. Since then, each time you've made a sound you've re-created yourself!

Over the centuries, we have developed an understanding of the transformative power of sound and have come to understand how, as a living force, sound also has the ability to transmute life. It can transform our thoughts and feelings and, therefore, the very substance and state of our bodies. For a simple illustration of this, think of how dramatically harsh the sound of a pneumatic drill or car horn can be when it shocks us from a moment of personal reflection. This radical understanding has led scientists to explore exciting new horizons, such as the development of sound wave instruments that have the power to transform cellular energy and, consequently, heal the human body.

Yet of all the sounds that exist, I believe the human voice is the most powerful. Its living, breathing, creative force gives us the ability to make wondrous changes in our thinking and feeling, our creating and constructing. For the power of our voice crystallizes thought, and so its energy may be used to transmute our outlook, attitude, beliefs, creativity, and physical presence; it transforms our lives. Think of the way a certain piece of music can have a profound effect on your mood. Now imagine that there is a far greater power within you, which is available at all times and which, when directed by you, can affect not only your mood but your entire outlook and belief about your personal power in the world. This instrument of sound you possess—your voice—can become your own liberating, creative, and life-changing force.

In subsequent chapters, I will take you on a journey of discovery to explore the power of your own voice, and show you how to harness and develop its potential in order to enrich, enchant, encourage, and ennoble your life. But first let me explain, briefly, the role of sound in the origin of the universe, and the extraordinary power of sound through the ages—in particular, the sound of the human voice.

In the Beginning, God said: "Let there be light and there was light..."

The ancient peoples of our planet believed that all creation was accomplished by sound and that the earth itself came into being through the power of sound; a sound that moved and still moves through every aspect of creation. They believed that this animating principle was the sound of God's voice.

As a result, human beings have always dedicated their voices to the veneration and glory of God as the prime creator. Through praise, petition, and participation, we have thrown up our voices in respect of the notion that: "In the beginning was the Word, and the Word was with God, and the Word was God." This statement resonates throughout all cultures in different forms. Through this resonance, I believe a collective belief cries out that the harmony of nature's sound is the source of all manifestation and the cause of all existence, and is, therefore, the only true medium between God and man, an indivisible connection between the creator and sound.

Man has named and known God in many forms. Indeed, the very word "human" is drawn from ancient words connected with the spirit of God. In the East, the sound of the outpouring breath *hu* is known as the spirit of all sounds and of all words. The sound *hu* in the word "human" means "the breath of spirit" (Sanskrit), while *mah* means "water" (Arabic). The Bible says: "Except a man be born of water and spirit, he cannot enter into the kingdom of heaven." Furthermore, in Eastern mysticism the word "human" illuminates two ideas within the character of human-ness: *hu* means "God" and *man* means "mind." The two words then fuse or transmute, indicating that God is within all beings, and that it is through humanity that God is known.

Ancient cultures knew this and celebrated their teachings through sacred and secular sound. They directed the resonance of their sacred harmonies with the energy of thought, inspired by their hearts. They believed that through sound the triple function of the eternal, the universal, and the individual were encapsulated within the fusion of past, present, and future, and that within this force lay the blueprint of humanity as an eternal force.

The Big Bang Theory

The world of science confirms the role of sound in the origin of our world: the theory referred to as the "Big Bang" supports the beliefs of peoples throughout history.

The foremost scientific intellects of today suggest that a fusion of mass energy must have taken place to create the stars and galaxies. I imagine that this original explosion would have been like a colossal firework display, an alchemy of divine proportion, as light, through an interplay with darkness, created color, then sound. Here is a simple illustration of this. If you hang a crystal prism in a south-facing window, a moment of pure magic occurs when sunlight pours through the prism. The effect is an immediate explosion of color in the form of the primary rainbow colors throughout the room. The power of the sun is the energy that begins this creation, the vibration of life as we see it, and as such it has been worshipped by human beings since the beginning of time. Molecular physics proclaims that from the sun arises light, and from light arises color, and then sound. As with all things, human beings were created from a continuum of rapidly moving light, color, and sound.

Just as sunlight through a prism produces seven rays of rainbow color, so our voice produces different vibrations, or tones. In later chapters we will discover how to tune into our signature note, the note that exists at the center of our compass or vocal range. When we shine the inspirational light of breath through this note, resonance sounds out as an amplification from which harmonics are produced that make up our individual timbre—this is heard by all of us and can also be imaged by a few. It is a force of immense power.

The Energy of Sound

The energy of sound is felt through the vibrations of pitch and resonance. Imagine throwing a stone into a pool of water and watching the ripples spreading out from the point at which the stone entered the water. Resonance works in the same way—oscillating out in waves from the point of origin.

The laws of physics teach us that life is composed of atoms that contain electrons and protons— electrically and magnetically charged energy particles that are in constant motion. When we hear a sound, every cell within our body resonates in response, creating a similar movement rather like fusion. The same thing happens in the "atoms" of inanimate objects. We all know the story of the highly trained vocalist who can smash a crystal glass with her voice. When the frequency of the sung note finds a harmonic balance with the vibration of the glass, the object rings or resonates with its note. However, if the singer increases the volume of the note, the note's force will upset the acoustic balance of the glass, and the crystal shatters.

Even more incredibly, sound also has the power to transform our psyche, which leads to changes within our soma. One of the most fascinating stories I have heard about the transformative power of sound was told to me by a survivor of the Holocaust. This man was interned in a Nazi German concentration camp during the Second World War. To alleviate their suffering and to mollify their captors, a number of the imprisoned men who had been musicians and singers organized themselves into a group. They prepared and performed some of the romantic Italian operas of the nineteenth century— works by Puccini, Verdi, and Rossini—as a number of the men were highly accomplished musicians, who before the war had played in some of Europe's finest orchestras. These men perfected their music-making to such a degree that they were considered superlative by the Nazis. However, an interesting phenomenon occurred. Over a period of time, the young men who sang the female roles in soprano or falsetto voices ceased growing facial hair and started to develop partial breast formations. This was, of course, alarming, but as soon as they stopped singing the female roles in emotionally charged scenarios, the physiological changes reverted. These young men, who identified so profoundly with their roles, were actually affecting their body's hormonal equilibrium.

What this amazing story illustrates is how profoundly the voice can affect the physiology of the body. What we often forget is that our everyday, mundane lives are filled with sayings that reflect this connection. For example, the phrase "a problem shared is a problem halved" implies that often, even if the problem still exists after talking it through with a friend or trusted counsel, we feel much better simply for talking about it—ergo, there is a release in speaking; we are changed by making sound.

Or the time-worn adage: "Sticks and stones will break your bones, but words will never hurt you." Have you ever thought how inaccurate this phrase is? Words can be just as hurtful as being physically hit. We have all felt love in the words spoken by a gentle caregiver and felt the hurt in words that are filled with injury and insult, which can be just as violent as being hit by a stick.

Sound and Matter

The theory of sound affecting matter has been investigated since the end of the nineteenth century and has resulted in major scientific achievements.

The Swiss doctor and engineer Hans Jenny spent many hours researching the effect of sound on matter during the early part of the twentieth century. He collected a series of different substances, such as powder and iron filings, and then introduced different sound vibrations to the surfaces on which the heaps of matter were exposed. When this occurred, the amorphous substances turned into intricate shapes and patterns that echoed the organic shapes found in the natural world, such as the leaf of a plant, the spiraling interior of a shell, or the patterns of snowflakes. What he found was that the stronger and more persistent the sound, the more precise the effect of the pattern. The use of inorganic matter to create organic shapes illuminated an interesting reality: the matter was not alive but assumed the features of life when affected by sound.

Dr Jenny called this pioneering work Cymatics, from the Greek *Kyma*, which means "to wave." Since the time of these discoveries, many areas of the scientific establishment have utilized his theories. For example, the development of ultrasound has become a well-established tool in the field of medicine, in particular to determine the welfare of unborn babies. Sound waves are passed over the pregnant mother's stomach and calibrated by computer technology, so that the image of the unborn child can be seen.

In addition, Dr. Sir Peter Guy Manners invented a Cymatics instrument that applies sound directly to the body. Harmonically related tones resonate with the imbalanced organ or tissue, thereby restoring balance and well-being. This sophisticated instrument identifies the particular sound frequency required for each imbalanced organ or muscular locus, and Dr Manners believes that any organic imbalance can be "reharmonized."

Another process confirming these hypotheses is known as "entrainment." This involves the sourcing of powerful vibrations and introducing them to an energy vibrating at a lower frequency. Interestingly, the lesser frequency is penetrated and absorbed by the greater host frequency, reforming the initial status of the energy. When this notion is posited in reference to Dr Manners' theory all becomes clear, as it would seem that the unbalanced organ (the lesser frequency) has "cell potential" that takes on the resonance of the greater frequency, thus restoring balance and health.

Architects and structural engineers design and build bridges or multistory buildings using entrainment. A study is carried out to find the resonance frequency of the building's structure, so that if it is adversely affected by high-velocity energies, such as wind or earthquake, flexible architectural features can be included within the structure to limit possible damage.

Entrainment has been occurring for centuries. In the Old Testament there is the story of Joshua, who destroyed the city walls of Jericho using sound. Joshua and his people circled the city walls seven times, and while seven priests played on rams' horns, the people made a great sound and the walls came tumbling down. Joshua and his people knew the note of the walls. Modern engineers have also puzzled over how the Egyptians were able to move the vast stones used to build the pyramids. A theory has been put forward that the ancient Egyptians organized choirs of thousands to move solid matter—the stones were levitated by sound vibrations.

Oral Traditions

Teachings about the power of sound have been passed from generation to generation through the influence of oral traditions: channels of repetitive narration arising from the collective psyche and used to unify the experience of life. In all parts of the world and in every language the human impulse to tell stories developed the power of these oral traditions. Over eons of time stories, poems, myths, and songs were passed down the ancestral line, expressing the essence of collective force that exists within each society and maintains the power of its cultural truth.

Through the Greek melodists, Mediterranean troubadours, Andalusian flamenco Gypsies, French jongleur minstrels, Celtic bards, African griots, Norse skalds, and Navajo singers, the power to teach, heal, and raise consciousness through the voice has been kept alive. Ancient peoples knew instinctively that the power of sound could create and destroy. When the human voice expresses wisdom, truth, and love, miracles can happen. This power is increased when other voices meet the solo voice in empathy and a joint intention is created; we call this synergy. People sang or chanted as they collectively labored, transforming the intensity of the physical activity into a continuous, rhythmic vibration of synchronized movement and fellowship. In short, when they sang as they worked, energy was created; the sound played a powerful role in helping the work along.

In the modern world we have lost much of this understanding. Today, most people are unaware or simply ignore the significance of their voice, or indeed the power of sound within their lives. We rarely sing or tell stories together. Yet singing retunes our personal vibration to that of our tribe, the singular dissolving into the collective and creating a feeling of unity, mutual strength, energy, and pride. Our national anthems are examples of this. Or think of the Welsh singing their national song "Men of Harlech" at Cardiff Arms Park for a rugby final. These vibrations proclaim the very essence of Welshness, reinforcing individual harmony and shared nationhood as the sung tones penetrate deeper and deeper into the collective psyche.

I believe that one of the major reasons why society has become so disenchanted is simply because we have lost the opportunity to sing, to chant, to use our voices as channels. Instead, we tolerate the noise of machines, piped "muzak," or personal stereos in our workplaces, all of which move the individual into a singular experience of inner mind space, which is diametrically opposed to the shared uplifting experience of the laborers singing together.

From Being to Doing

Over the past two or three centuries, many in the West have moved away from the force of "being," as we have become driven by the necessity of "doing." Consequently, the organic process of sounding the heart's joy, which occurred naturally through the ages, has been altered, and our voices merely convey information, moving from the heart's feeling center to the head's thinking center. Through this, our connection with the blueprint or "primal note" of our ancestors has become suppressed, and with it our ability to express ourselves fully and freely.

The advent of literacy changed the face of history, as the written word began to take over from the spoken word. Through the invention of the printing press and the development of rationalistic intellect, man became valued for his thinking process only, and the great oral traditions began to slowly dwindle. Now only a few indigenous cultures value the power of the human voice alone, speaking human stories.

The Pueblo Indians of New Mexico and Arizona, some of the oldest settled Native American peoples, believe that if the sounds of the human voice are written their power is lost. They believe that by writing these sounds "down" the vibrations of life become solidified and memory controlled—that sound energy made solid in print will merely reflect itself and will no longer convey the sacred message of life. Their ancient languages— Tiwa, Tewa, Towa, Zuni, Keresan, Hopi, etc.—are still only spoken not written down.

Similarly the Kogi Indians of South America do not have a written language. Their belief is that to write puts the power of the life force in a space between memory and possibility, between past and future, and in so doing the present is effectively extinguished.

Yet in the West, not only has the printed word become ubiquitous but technological forms of communication, such as television and computers, have arisen to convey information through pictures. Therefore, the importance of hearing the spoken word has substantially altered.

As we begin the twenty-first century, we are becoming more aware of the colossal imbalances that exist in both ourselves and our world. The core energies that exist within us and our environment, defined by the Chinese as Yin and Yang, are severely out of balance—the Yang "doing," or "masculine energy," has become far too dominant in proportion to the Yin "being," or "feminine energy."

The result is that our living functions are reduced to the action of the "do-er." The "doing" impulse is the energy we use to move forward in life and assert ourselves in the world. This impulse can be the source of great courage and expertise, but when we function through it in isolation we allow our lives to become devoid of feeling, operating in a "non-present," automatic-pilot fashion. We are simply preoccupied by the ends that need to be gained, rather than the means by which we move toward those ends. As a result of this preoccupation with the "do-er," we have unbalanced the "be-er" aspect of our nature—the instinctual feminine impulse that creates the force of receiving, yielding, loving, and nurturing. If this essential principle is ignored or stifled we are in danger of becoming hardened.

I Think Therefore I am:
Cogito Ergo Sum

During the Middle Ages in Europe the official doctrine taught in every university was that the earth was a living planet and all living things were of God's creation. Each aspect of nature was animate and filled with the breath of the holy spirit, which meant that everything had a soul.

However, during the Protestant Reformation of the sixteenth century vast changes took place, and the natural world became devoid of its spiritual power. Nature was seen in a new way, merely to be used by man as he saw fit. This led, in turn, to the mechanistic revolution, confirmed by Rene Descartes in 1619, when he envisioned a world governed by mathematical principles and defined man purely in terms of his thinking capacity: *Cogito Ergo Sum*.

What followed was the Age of Enlightenment, the Industrial Revolution, the rapid rise of literacy, and eventually the advent of mass media and the info-tech highway. Consequently, our voices took residence in our heads, producing effects such as the soundbite—a simple, limited thought containing nothing but a single point of news. We became conditioned to the attitude: "I must do this now, and preferably as quickly as possible!"

Restricting Our Voice

This domination of "doing" over "being" has moved us away from our instinctive and feeling responses. As a result we tend to live more in our heads than in our bodies, inhibiting the fullness of feeling in our voices and unconsciously creating a belief that thought is superior to feeling. As a consequence, our children have grave difficulty reading or remembering the great works of literature, but rather choose to watch television or "chat" on the Internet or through abbreviated text messages—functions that stifle the spoken word. We only connect with sound feelings when we are moved beyond ourselves by extreme situations that affect our emotional or physical state, when passion takes us into our gut, emotional center, viscera, solar plexus, or heart. When this happens, our response is to suddenly make pure organic sound, releasing emotional energy. Think of the whoop of joy, the cry of despair, the shout of excitement we all experience on rare occasions. When this happens we move from conceptual into experiential, from head into body fullness, from rational into irrational, from conscious into unconscious, and from automatic-pilot into "present state" behavior. We are moved into our primal core, so that the totality of our being is made audible, often in very primitive ways.

Despite these effects, so many of our truly natural sounds are impossible to suppress. Even when we don't speak, our bodies make sounds of digestion: rumbling, swallowing, passing wind, gurgling, gulping, lip-smacking, teeth-clashing, and so on. When we breathe, we snort, sneeze, wheeze, sniff, pant, and snore. When we move, our joints crack, feet pound, hands tap, fingers snap, jaws click, teeth grind, and clothes rustle. In short, we are very noisy creatures. We give away our feelings when we moan, groan, grunt, shush, snicker, hiss, giggle, laugh, sigh, and yawn to indicate pain, pleasure, sorrow, joy, and the rest of the kaleidoscope of human feelings. If we suppress feeling by holding back our tears, we become extremely withheld, and this leads to the inevitable mind/body complications, such as ill health, unhappiness, and emotional constipation.

The Head and Heart Connection

The impact of the cerebral nature of shifting our voices from our bodies and hearts into our heads has been enormous and has had a dramatic effect on our physical lives. Few of us now speak with the conviction of the true, rich-rooted voice that we are capable of using. Instead this quality of voice lies suppressed or unremembered within us, smothered by the conditioning, education, beliefs, and attitudes with which we have been restricted.

Yet the physiology of the human body and the functioning of the voice within it clearly illustrates the "head and heart" connection that is the essence of a truly healthy voice. The voice is located in the larynx, which sits in the neck, symbolizing a passageway between head and heart and a conduit between mind and body. To open its potential power we need a stimulant, the breath, which is our very life force. Breath becomes physical in the torso and stomach, where we fully experience the feelings and sensations of life and all its creativity, and so our voice becomes an expressive instrument, connecting us with the essence and feeling of our being. In these moments we revolutionize ourselves into a potential balance, whereby Descartes' definition of man changes to become "I think *and feel,* and therefore I am what I truly am."

As we make a sound it travels through vibrations we know as sound waves. These sound waves are picked up by those around us. But while we hear the sounds others make, we also feel them. When we sound, the note we produce has a sympathetic vibration that we call resonance. Resonance, the amplification of the original note, is affected by the size and shape of the cavities within our bodies, through which the sound is shaped. Thus we each have our own particular and totally individual resonance. When we speak or sound from the heart, other people "feel" us as well as hear our intention.

When we move the voice solely into our head, it is difficult to express and reveal subtle feelings fully; they become extreme and withheld, and so we witness other people's emotional process by what is not revealed, rather than what is. The good news is that, since the 1960s, as a consequence of Eastern thought corridors opening into the West, there has been a shift in consciousness toward a better balance. We in the West owe much to the lasting impact that Eastern healing and energy centering techniques has had on our culture. Who has not heard of yoga, tai chi, acupuncture, shiatsu, feng shui, or transcendental meditation? All are disciplines that aim to train individual consciousness to a state of perfect spiritual insight and, therefore, union with the universal spirit—human meets divine.

Remembering Our Note

As Western societies shift toward a rebalance between the doing and being aspects of our natures, so I believe it is increasingly vital for each of us to find our true voice. The need to discover the joy and depth of creating our voice from within the fullness of our being is powerful, and is entirely possible. Each one of us has simply "unremembered" our primal note, the sound kept alive for so long through the songlines of our oral traditions. This primal sound is stored within our cellular memory, awaiting a time when we can rediscover its sensation and fulfil its promise.

In Conclusion...

When you rediscover your ability to speak from the heart you profoundly affect not only the quality and resonance of your voice but the way in which you communicate with others. You will be heard more easily, convey your words more effectively, and communicate at a far deeper and more heartfelt level. Those around you will automatically be drawn to you, sensing your authenticity and whole-heartedness. Your body, mind, and spirit will become more balanced, and you will find it easier to live in the truth of present-moment consciousness.

CHAPTER 2

†HE VOICE MASK

The soul reveals itself through the voice.
—*HENRY WADSWORTH LONGFELLOW*

Our voice is the inspirational, vital force of our being, and therefore one of the truest mirrors of our inner life, health, stability, joy, pain, or disinterest. When we listen to another person's voice, we immediately know whether they are at ease or tense, joyful or angry, feeling open to communication or closed. The voice is the blueprint of one's psycho-physical nature, as well as being the channel for one's integrity.

In the ancient Greco-Roman world, there was a belief that if the individual spoke with *integritas,* or integrity, they indicated how sound, or complete, they were. It was important that the individual be fully integrated, physically, mentally, and emotionally, and so live the "sincere or honest" path. Interestingly, the word *sincere* actually means "without wax." During the time of the Italian Renaissance, when masterpieces such as Michelangelo's *David* were created from marble, if the stone was blemished, wax was used to fill the offending cracks, concealing any errors and returning the work to seeming perfection. Therefore, to be without imperfection was to be "without wax," or *sin-cere.*

The tone of our voice often tells more about us than the words we choose. For example, the healthy, well-balanced speaker has a well-modulated, clear vocal richness, as though they are singing with joy as they speak. Whereas the voice of someone who is ill at ease, unwell, or depressed can be constrained, tense, or introverted. When we manifest the latter state of being, our jaw tightens and the tone of voice becomes "cracked," as it is locked in the throat, as though we are sitting back on our voice to stop it from yielding forth our true nature. By way of illustration, think of the way a young adolescent sounds when they feel guilty or uncomfortable about a misdemeanor.

The voice we develop as we mature is not simply a "given" from birth. Rather, it is affected in its unfolding route to maturity by experiential, social, environmental, and cultural factors. In short, the adult voice has been subject to many different external influences, as well as being affected by

31

the internal choices we make as consciousness develops; these choices may be conscious or unconscious.

My belief is that many people in the West hide their true vocal richness behind a "mask"—a voice that has been adopted in order to convey an image that will be acceptable to society. The "voice mask" is like a protective outer layer that conceals the innermost quality of selfhood with all its attendant feeling. The "voice mask" may make the individual feel more socially acceptable or upwardly mobile. But, conversely, it may also leave the individual unhappy and dissatisfied, because on an instinctual level they know their true integrity, the truly authentic power of themselves, is being restricted. With the voice mask in place, they cannot speak out or allow their true selves to be shown, as "feeling" is imprisoned within.

Many of us begin to adopt a chosen voice from an early age as social influences and expectations let us know what we must do and be in order to "fit in." As a consequence, many of us are unconscious of the fact that we have a truer voice that has not been expressed. Take, for example, the stern male boss who feels insecure and so always appears aloof, stiff, and rigid. An individual like this may produce the overly "nasal" sound often created by those who look down their noses at other people—his jaw will probably be tense and the vowel tones clipped. Or the woman who stays at home seemingly trapped by her domestic life, who feels constricted or stifled and longs for the opportunity to fulfil herself beyond the limited world of the house. She may have a voice that is constrained and that reflects how she feels—unsupported and small. To speak is to proclaim ourselves in the world; once we have created in this way we may no longer hide.

In this chapter, I will outline the development of the voice and the conditions, influences, and choices that affect our voice from infancy through to adulthood. I will also ask you to listen to your own voice and to answer the question "What does your voice say about you?" so that we may create an understanding of how to speak and sound with a voice that feels authentic. Over the lintel of each door in the ancient world was inscribed: TO THY OWN SELF BE TRUE or KNOW THYSELF. This is the energy we will evoke through this chapter.

The Infant Voice

The unborn child in the watery world of its mother's womb hears through an acoustic sea of sound. This information arises from scientific examination proving that unborn infants also make sound as they float within the amniotic fluid. Fetuses, therefore, create vocal vibrations not unlike whales and dolphins, our fellow mammals who use sound waves and vibrational frequencies far above, or indeed below, the limits of human hearing. The sounds produced in this context are made more specific as water is a finely effective conductor of energy, assisting the ultrasonic vibrations used by sea mammals. When research was carried out to discover which sounds unborn babies respond to most, it was found, perhaps not surprisingly, that they prefer softer, more lyrical melodies that are similar to the "white noise" communicated through whale song.

The newborn baby is subject to a sea of sounds perhaps similar to the ones heard in the womb, meaning that sounds blend together, without any particular distinction or meaning. However, as the child grows, sounds quickly become more distinct, led by the voices of caregivers, which become the most important sounds in the infant's world. Mothers use soothing sounds to encourage their children and prepare the way for "talk." This is known as Motherese and is common in most of the world's cultures. The development of hearing and listening skills is associated with this vital, loving nourishment, like the vital nourishment suckled from breast or bottle.

This does not occur for the deaf child. If deafness is present at birth, children develop other sensory skills to compensate for the lack of sound awareness. For example, they often develop a stronger sense of smell, taste, sight, or touch and can "feel" sound through vibrations. Later, "verbally percussive sounds" are used to accompany the language of "signing" and to assist physical expression, while other subtle communication takes place on other sensory levels.

The Role of the Senses

The behavioral research of Neuro-Linguistic Programming (NLP), an advanced communications training process, has provided great insight into the way in which, through our "brain-language" faculties, we unconsciously choose words to filter and express our perception of the world. Simply put, we perceive the entire world through our senses, and in order to effectively communicate concepts we tend to use one sense more than the others, as indicated through our choice of words (see below).

If we are iconic or "visual" thinkers, we think in pictures and often use rapid-fire speech delivery while filtering images. During this process, the electrical frequency of the brain is very high, and consequently a lack of speech clarity can occur as we tend to breathe in the upper chest alone and, therefore, create physical tensions.

Conversely, kinesthetic people, who predominantly function through touch, have a flow of vocal energy that is often evenly modulated and which is supported by breath from a lower level within the abdominal area.

The lists below will give you an idea of the kinds of phrases chosen by people who function through each of the senses. Perhaps you will recognize yourself, or someone you know.

KINESTHETIC – OF TOUCH

I like the weight of that.
I feel what you mean.
He is a chip off the old block.
Just get to grips with it.
Get in touch with this.
Hang in there.
Now just hold on!

ICONIC – OF VISION

Beyond a shadow of a doubt.
He really got an eyeful.
From a bird's-eye view
We saw eye to eye.
Just picture what it would be like.
I take a dim view of that.
That's a sight for sore eyes.

AUDITORY – OF HEARING

Would you grant an audience?
Yes, as clear as a bell.
He really got an earful.
Would you give an account of?
Now hold your tongue.
I like the sound of that.
To tell the truth.

GUSTATORY AND OLFACTORY – OF TASTE AND SMELL

He gets right up my nose.
He's hanging around like a bad smell.
I really savored that idea.
That notion stinks!
Let me chew the idea over.

He blew that idea.
Stiff upper lip.

Sensory Crossover

Most children express an awareness of a subtle perceptual phenomenon known as synesthesia. This is a blending of the senses and is most frequently triggered by sound. For example, in hearing a piece of music, visual images, smell, or taste sensations can be evoked, tuning into memories that have often lain dormant for many years. When visiting a clothing store in the United States recently, I had an experience of my own synesthesia. I heard the sound created by the tread of someone ascending an iron staircase in the shop. Each footfall struck a different note, and I was instantly transported back to the childhood moment when I first heard a wonderful piece of music. The scene of my "inner vision" was filled with color, shape, and texture, and as soon as the moment passed I was left bathed in an echo of the memory and its significance.

Synesthesia is an instinctual and intuitive phenomenon. We almost all experience it as children, but as we grow up most of us lose awareness of this "sensory crossover," so that by the time we are adults we only have occasional vague recollections at times of heightened feeling. However, it is quite possible to recover the ability to experience synesthesia, simply by believing that it is possible and allowing ourselves time to experience it. For instance, many actors use techniques associated with "sense and emotional memory" in order to evoke powerful states of feeling as part of their characterization.

I once worked with a leading actor as he prepared to play Hamlet. Hamlet's character explores two primary states of feeling within the play. The first is deep melancholia, as a consequence of his father's death and the events that arise from the tragedy, while the second is a powerfully active determination to avenge his father's death, which occurs as a consequence of meeting his father's ghost. The ghost reveals that he was poisoned by his own brother who wished to become king in his stead and to marry the dead king's wife, Gertrude.

The sensitive actor I worked with found these emotional states difficult to create from his own experience and worried that he would not seem authentic in the part. For great actors it is important to create a sense of "truth" in their work, so that the audience can truly believe in it.

In this case, the actor was able to find the relevant emotions by remembering the loss he felt at the death of a dear friend and the anger he felt at the seeming futility of such a young death. By recalling the physical sensations and experiences he had gone through at the time, he was able to recapture what it felt like when the death occurred, and so sympathetically identified with Hamlet's state and felt authentic and credible as he prepared for the part.

Early Language

As infants grow and develop, their early knowing of sound changes and they begin to use formal language constructions. Speaking is a highly specialized skill, learned through contact with other social beings. Small children instinctually learn to use sound tone through imitating the pitch, resonance, and rhythm of those around them. So basic language structures grow.

An infant who is not spoken to, or who is isolated from speech, will experience profound difficulty in developing vocabulary and may not learn to speak at all. Children who suck dummies for prolonged periods can also develop speech difficulties, as indeed can those who are constantly shushed and told to be quiet. When the child's natural expression of sound is inhibited, tension is created and problems with expression and speech can arise.

While traveling through the Far and Middle East I have rarely heard or seen children discouraged from making sound. Babies in this part of the world seldom express discomfort or cry for attention, as they are constantly held and comforted by their mothers or other women within the home environment. The child is held against the body of the caregiver, allowing him or her to feel warmth and comfort. In other words, if the child yells for attention, attention is provided.

Today a vast range of sound options are available to the growing child, as a consequence of our sophisticated communication systems. Yet language skills are still modeled on the words, grammar, and syntax offered by those in the immediate environment. Language skills enable the child to travel into the world and communicate successfully with other members of society.

Puberty

In general, young children are not self-conscious or aware of their own voices. They simply make sound as they respond to their own feelings. But as they grow older and enter into more formal modes of education, they slowly become aware of the way they sound and how they are identified by it. This specifically occurs during puberty, as a result of the hormonal changes that take place.

As our voice awareness grows we shift into a sense of our personality. The word comes from the Latin *persona,* which means "through sounds." This gives us an indication of the vital role sound plays in forming the personality; the way we sound creates our conscious individuality, as our voice gives our consciousness evidence of itself. The consciousness of our voice, particularly when unmasked, allows the "knower" to become known to him or herself.

This is true of both vocal tone and the words we use. Think of the buzz words and slang terms that gain teenagers' credibility within their peer groups. These soundbytes emerge from the need to be accepted and honored by members of the immediate tribe. Puberty is the time when, moving toward adulthood, our identity is confirmed by society or our social unit. Throughout history, cultures around the world have conducted rites of passage as a means for their young men and women to formally achieve adulthood. These initiation ceremonies allow young adults to gain communion with respected elders and to enter mature levels of tribal identity. Many still exist today, including the sacrament of confirmation in the Christian faith, the bar mitzvah of Judaism, the sweat lodge and vision quest of the Amerindian tribes, and the Amrit Chhakna of Sikhism. What all these social initiations have in common is the enactment of sound ceremonies in which sacred pronouncements are spoken or chanted to initiate conscious awareness of the fact that life is changing or maturing, and therefore must be respected.

Social Conditioning

Our social conditioning influences our voice and speech more than anything else. Our voice is shaped by social factors that affect the way we allow ourselves to be heard, and by the way other members of our tribe or social group give us permission to sound.

We can only produce the sounds that we hear, and so as young people we are influenced by the voices, pronunciation, vowel tones, sense of rhythm, and energy of the people around us. Similarly, if we are encouraged to speak or express the feelings that arise within us, we express them with great ease. However, if parent and school are sternly authoritarian and restrictive, children often find it difficult to express themselves and to lift up their voices and speak or sing—to sound their truth in the world.

It follows that if a person has difficulty in perceiving pitch or singing in tune, this often says more about their lack of personal power than the accuracy of their pitching or hearing. When children first attempt formal speaking or singing in school and are told by teachers that their sound is wrong, this creates confusion or a lack of confidence, and as a result inaccurate pitching; as the neural pathways are disturbed through hurt feelings, it is difficult to be brave and sound. Similarly, rapid and imprecise speech and an inability to express ideas clearly are often the result of early disempowerment, rather than the more easily associated "laziness."

Disempowerment brings with it heavily camouflaged frustration and anger, so that the individual becomes tight-lipped and clench-jawed. Think back to the last time you engaged in conflict with a child under your care. If they did not wish to engage, what did you see happening in their jaw? Similarly, look at the clenched jaws of metropolitan people traveling home on the bus or train during rush hour. The frustrations and unexpressed notions of the day are held tightly in their faces and jaws, bringing with them tight-throated vowels, upper chest breathing, and voiced consonants that are often very nasal.

Try squeezing the back of your tongue up against the rear of the roof of your mouth; keep the tip against the lower teeth—not pressed, just in light contact. Try saying *GEE, GEE, GEE*, tightening your jaw as you do it. Then relax. Then do the same thing with your jaw free and heavy, and the back of your tongue free and heavy, and notice the huge difference. Now repeat the exercise with your hand on your upper chest. The first time you will feel little resonance in your chest, but the second, as you release your jaw and tongue, a tremendous amount of resonance will occur. Try this again saying "Hello, my name is… !" and notice the difference. Does it remind you of anyone?

This is a clear illustration of how we close off sound from our bodies when we are tense.

In a very broad sense, our social and physical circumstances condition the way we live our lives. The food we eat, the buildings in which we live and work, the lay of the land, the climate, and the clothes we wear, the familiarity of our tribe—all these influences affect who we are on an outer and inner plane and, consequently, our voice. One of the clearest social references for this is the way in which the current sound of Estuary English has developed since the period after the Second World War. During the immediate post-war years, after the East End Dockland area and City of London were devastated by Hitler's bombing campaign, many of the inhabitants moved to the mouth of the River Thames. East Enders who spoke with a Cockney dialect moved north or south into Essex or Kent, causing the indigenous sounds of the Southend and Chelmsford folk to mutate into the now familiar sound of the Essex accent. Similarly, the Kent accent shifted under the influence of the laid-back tone that has become common on the Isle of Thanet.

The social conditioning of Estuary English is now rife throughout southern England, so much so that it is considered to be the norm by many people—the sound of Standard English, so common during the 1940s, 1950s, and 1960s, has radically changed. We human beings consciously or unconsciously sound the way our tribes sound.

For the young acting student, this can be an issue of great conflict. For example, a young actor from Rochester with an Estuary accent would, on entering drama school, need to learn a Standard English or received pronunciation accent. This would eventually allow the young actor to work in all mediums and to undertake both contemporary and classical work. It is a *lingua franca* for most actors, making the culture of the play's context clear, rather than obscuring it through various dialects. The importance of the word must impinge on the listener rather than the way the word sounds. In a sense, actors are classless citizens, which is essential if they are to hold a "mirror up to nature," and by that I mean all natures. For the young actor starting at drama school, this can create huge problems, as they often feel disloyal to their social group. I often hear actors saying that they were considered "posh" for speaking Standard English when they returned home. In a sense, our social group gives us "permission" to speak with a certain tone, and this can be hard to resist until the individual can break into full personal power and not feel fractured by others' opinions.

The Influence of Landscape on the Voice

The landmass on which we live and breathe has a powerful effect on us. My belief is that the climate, terrain, habitat, air quality, and energy of our landscape affect not just the way we think and behave but our sound-making, too.

The people of the Welsh valleys offer a wonderful example of this. They generally use lilting sound patterns that reflect the undulating nature of the terrain on which they live. Diametrically opposed to this is the sharp, glottal sound pattern of the city dweller, whose landscape is often unremitting concrete.

An eminent Canadian music professor conducted an experiment with college students in both North America and Europe in order to identify the effect of landscape on our sound-making. When the students were asked to hum the first sound that came to them, the North Americans spontaneously produced the musical note B flat. The Europeans produced G sharp. The music professor then observed that in North America the electrical grid operates on an alternating current of sixty cycles per second, which directly calibrates with B flat, while in Europe the electrical grid operates at fifty cycles per second, which calibrates with G sharp. What this illustrates is that the electricity of each country has a profound effect on the physical life of each person—in other words, we are psychologically affected by our physical circumstances.

Living as we do in an age of global warming, air quality and climatic conditions are increasingly poor. Over the past decade there has been an increase in asthma and other similar respiratory illnesses. Our vital breath force has been affected and, as breath gives life to sound, so have our voices. The result is that many people hold their breath and sound, creating tensions that constrain their vocal expression.

Geopathic energy is another huge influence on the way we live our lives. Geopathic or geomantic energy is the potent natural energy of our world, known to many peoples as Gaia or Earth Mother, and in particular the powerful network of energy lines—*ley* lines, from an old Saxon word meaning "fire" or "light"—that course through the physical landscape of our planet. These lines are similar to the arteries within our bodies and are currents of electromagnetic energy. They are not unlike the meridian lines of the subtle-physical body identified in Eastern medical practices such as acupuncture, shiatsu, and chi kung.

When ley lines converge they create tremendously strong resonance, which forms into centers of great power. These centers were venerated by ancient peoples as sacred. The "crack," or fissure, at Delphi in Greece is such a site. It is a natural fissure breaking the earth's surface, and was held by the ancient Greeks to be a place of great prophecy: a temple of Apollo was constructed at this place, where an oracle was consulted. So important was this site that it was revered as the very center of the ancient world.

In northern Europe, Chartres Cathedral in France is also a place of rare energy, and like many other Christian cathedrals is devoted to the Virgin Mary. Prior to the advent of Christianity, the earth site at Chartres was a center of great pilgrimage, specifically to venerate the Divine Female. There are many other such venerable centers of earth power throughout the world, such as Machu Picchu in Peru, Giza in Egypt, and Glastonbury or Avebury Henge in the United Kingdom. Since early times there has been the awareness that these centers are connected with divine force, and people have visited to praise, to enchant, to beseech, and to evoke God-like powers to intervene and bring about a successful outcome of life issues.

Variable Factors That Affect the Voice

So far we have looked at developmental, educational, social, and geographic factors that affect the kind of voice we may form. However, there are other, more variable factors that also affect our voice. These include stress, trauma, illness—in short, the negative effluent of our physical, emotional, and mental state.

The breathy voice of the shy, withheld person, the cracking voice of someone in fear or under stress, the indistinct tonal color of the insecure, and the booming blast of the bombast are all clear illustrations of a person who is not emotionally or physically balanced and in full health. Similarly, if a person places their voice solely in the head a "cerebral" quality is communicated rather than the rich, passionate warmth of emotional resonance that is heard from one who speaks from the heart.

The voice reflects our innermost feelings. In my work, I often meet people who are possessed by great inner turmoil because they cannot produce the sound they desire. This is largely because they have unresolved painful feelings created by past experiences and are out of balance with themselves. Sometimes, to establish the reason behind the problem, a journey into the psyche is necessary, though a therapeutic journey of this kind should not be taken lightly, and only with a qualified practitioner.

It is interesting to note that the psychoanalyst Carl Jung referred to the throat as the "ring of fear," an observation derived from his compassionate, scholarly, and therapeutic interaction with human trauma. He was referring to the closing of the sphincter muscles in the trachea, larynx, and pharynx that occurs during trauma.

Obviously, when we are physically challenged by stress or trauma our voice reflects the internal pressure that we are experiencing. If an individual is in pain, the whole body contracts on a muscular level. It is difficult to breathe fully and deeply, and as a result the voice becomes thin or shrill, existing in the head and not the area where the pain is felt.

In my private practice I was once sought out by a woman named Anne. She was a brave thirty-year-old, paralyzed from the waist down, who lived her life in a wheelchair. Despite this, Anne had created a life of almost complete independence, living alone, driving her own automatic car, and working for a major charity. However, as a result of her paraplegia she found it difficult to feel the sensations of breath support, and so her voice was weak, tight, and nasal. In addition, when she spoke, she unconsciously chose very short sentences, rather like a newsreader's "bullet-points," which finished in a minor key on a falling inflection. This she felt was depressing to listen to.

I was able to reassure her that plenty could be done, and we set to work. When we tried opening the breath to fuller, longer sentences it brought up a great deal of emotion for her, and she often wept. I asked her how young she felt when this occurred and she said, "Thirteen." It emerged that this was when she had been in a serious car accident. She had been the only survivor and her spinal cord had been almost fully severed.

Anne had been successfully rehabilitated, and after a long time spent in hospital had moved to live with her grandparents, her parents being stationed abroad with the British Diplomatic Service. Both her grandparents, while warm and affectionate, were deaf, and so she spent large amounts of time in silence, in a sense holding back the vocal expression of her terrible trauma. The falling inflection in her speech came about at this time. It was an unconscious "whine" for attention.

When this story had been fully uncovered, and with the help of breathing and sound exercises, Anne was once more able to elongate her breath into sentences and to use a downward inflection rather than a fall at the end of each phrase.

Inflections are the tonal patterns we use to communicate sense through the stressing of words. Today, they are often chaotic in young people, who can be unconsciously indecisive about their lives and, therefore, use rising inflections on every statement, almost as though they are speaking in questions.

Changes in the physiology of the body can also affect the voice.

My experience shows that many women notice a pronounced change in the quality of their voice during menstruation, particularly those who are professional singers or speakers. Women in these professions often feel this change to be negative, as the efficacy of their tone is not fully present while the vocal cords are thick with mucus. This is because the opening of the vocal cords, the glottis, has very similar biological tissue to the opening of the cervix, and during menstruation the fluid discharge in each organ often corresponds. Some female opera singers will have written into their contracts that they will not sing during menses. Similarly, leading performers will avoid singing immediately after a long air journey. A day or two of recovery is necessary to undo the physiological pressure changes and dehydration that often take place during air travel. As we all know, our voices always sound dry, croaky, or subtly uncomfortable after long periods of travel, as our whole being fluctuates in dealing with the pressure changes, the persistent noise, and any of the other stresses that accompany traveling by air.

What Does Your Voice Say about You?

Your voice is your identity in sound. It is far more than just a means with which to communicate your thoughts and feelings; it is the expression of your integrity and individuality in the world. Think about the following questions:

What does your voice tell those around you?
Which tone do you use most frequently?
Which words do you choose?
How would others describe your voice?

Try the following exercise, writing down your thoughts and responses to it.

EXERCISE — GETTING TO KNOW YOUR VOICE

Spend a day listening to your own voice. Notice your tone and words. Then write a brief description of your voice and the way you use it. Alternatively, record yourself speaking while you discuss a life issue with your family or friends. Answer the following questions.

1. Does your voice sound flat and dull, or lively and energetic?
2. Are you expressive, or do you seldom change your tone?
3. Do you mumble, speak fast, hesitate, or seldom stop?
4. Are you loud or soft? Do you often sound angry, uncertain, timid, bossy, or confident?
5. Do you shout, plead, or give orders?
6. Do you get the response you would like from others without raising your voice?

7. Do you leave out final consonants in the words that you choose?
8. Does speaking more loudly feel as though it strains your voice?
9. Do you feel self-conscious about your voice?
10. What would you change about your voice?

These are all questions we rarely think about. We simply use our voices without noticing *how* we use them, so a day of self-observation can be very enlightening.

Most of us would like to change or improve something about our voice. I will guide you in developing the voice you wish to have, the voice that feels truly and authentically yours, and which expresses clearly what you want to say to the world. I will show you how to look behind the "mask" of the voice you have chosen for yourself, to release and rejoice in your true vocal potential.

In the next chapter we will begin by looking in depth at the wondrous energy of the breath, an energy that, when used effectively, will prove to be the key to all vocal change.

In Conclusion ...

Your voice has been changing and developing since you were born, and will have been affected by the landscape and community in which you lived and the beliefs you have about yourself and your place in the world. Yet, despite the many outer influences, your voice is still the key to your soul, the unique measure of who you are, your identity in sound.

If, like so many people in the West, you have "masked" your true voice in a protective outer layer of what you feel is acceptable, suppressing and denying its full potential, then now is the time to cast off the mask and reveal the vocal richness and integrity that lies beneath.

Let me guide you, step by step, in discovering, exploring, and delighting in the voice that is truly yours. Transform your voice, and with it your life.

CHAPTER 3

BREATH AS CREATOR

The breath of life is the nectar drunk by the gods.
—*PLATO*

Our every activity in life depends on the ability to breathe. When we are born, the first independent action we achieve is to breathe in, and the last action we engage in at the end of life is to breathe out. Breath is the very measure of our lives. Yet in between birth and death, most of us take the air that moves through our nostrils and mouths completely for granted.

Breath is far more than a simple movement of air; our whole life depends on the rhythm of breath, whether it be the beating of our heart or the multiple rhythms and pulsations of our biochemistry. We can exist without food or even water for days, but if we are disconnected from breath we perish within minutes. Breath is the vital force that keeps us alive, nurtures our bodies, and connects us with all the other beings on our planet with whom we share breath. Breath is the flow of consciousness that emanates from the source and spreads to all things; it is a vast current of force, an energy that flows through everything in the cosmos. Yet few in the West are conscious of the breath's potential power to nourish, energize, and create anew that which we prize as most sacred—life itself.

In Britain, eight million people exercise each day, most of them without recognizing the power of breath to enhance and energize action and effort. Yet by harnessing the force of our breath we can create inner harmony, connecting mind, body, and spirit. Breath empowers, integrates, permeates, penetrates, invigorates, heals, and absorbs. It is within the very center of the process of conscious breathing that the secret power of the voice can be found. If the breath has length and breadth, the voice becomes fully empowered, as does the life of the individual. In order to explore your voice's potential we must begin with your breath.

Later in this chapter I will give you what I have discovered to be the easiest and most accurate breathing exercise possible—a means to improve your health, open your voice, and connect with your innermost being and creativity. Before we reach this, though, I will explain the connection between the breath and the soul; in short, the ancient beliefs about the power of breath, which are still potent and effective in our lives today.

Breath and the Soul

Breathing is known to be air breathed in and out. The medical terms we use for this wavelike action are inspiration and expiration: breathing in oxygen and breathing out carbon dioxide as waste. At the same time, what is interesting is that we use these words in other contexts.

Inspiration arises from the Latin root *inspirare,* meaning "to be influenced by the Divine"; expiration means "to breathe out," or "terminate life through the out-breath." The implications of this are clear. Once breathing becomes conscious, we open ourselves to an inspirational energy of divine order. Ancient peoples believed breath to be the animating principle behind all creation. Breath is the very self of man, and, therefore, the very soul of being is to be found in breath. In the East, the science of breath has been taught alongside the science of the mind for centuries.

Breath is known as "life force" in the West, transforming into the *prana* of India, the *chi* of China, and the *ki* of Japan. In Eastern yogic practice, it is believed that the energy of the breath was first derived from the serpent of the Kundalini energy, which is the vital creative force that waits to be awakened within our bodies, normally coiled within the base of our spines. The serpent Kundalini is the symbol of true wisdom, as we see in the image of Shiva, Lord of the Yogis, who is often depicted with a serpent wrapped around his neck. The serpent is also seen in the Judeo-Christian Bible as the creative force that tempts Eve into eating the fruit of the Tree of Knowledge.

Yoga is a particularly rich physical discipline through which to connect mind and body with universal spirit. Within yogic discipline lies the belief that breath is not merely a science but a sacred process. Therefore, it is only when breath harmonizes the flow of energy within the meditation and physical postures of yoga that it is possible to truly attain spiritual perfection.

In China, the energy practices of tai chi chuan and chi kung align the physical, emotional, mental, and spiritual bodies within us. Similarly in the Japanese tradition, *ki* is accessed within *reiki*, a profound healing process in which the universal force is channeled through the body of the practitioner into the body of the person requiring healing.

The Key to Balance

For the yogi and sufi, breath is the key to all balance, concentration, and wisdom. Within the Buddhist tradition, the activity of the mind is placed under the mantle of the breath. It is taught that with every breath one inhales the consciousness of the Divine. This is the only gain there ever is, and every breath taken without this consciousness is the only loss.

Many people are so absorbed in the petty things of daily life that they rarely give a thought to the importance and significance of breath. Their hearts are kept closed to this awareness until the body becomes so taxed by physical exertion that breathlessness creeps in, and with it ill health.

There is a truth increasingly accepted in the West and long expressed in the East that "thought creates reality": the thoughts we create in our mind in turn create the reality of our existence. With this knowledge comes power. If we breathe consciously, focusing our thoughts through the rhythm of our breath, the breath becomes a powerful energy for creation, inspiration, and change.

Breath creates vibrations and it is these waves that become energized by thought, carrying intention from one person to another. If thought power is strong and the breath of sound rich, then the wave is strongest. Within this process a balance must always be established; that is, to give and to receive. As we breathe in, we receive the thoughts and impressions of the world around us, and as we breathe out we send ourselves out into the world. If we feel the world as a hostile place, then we do not breathe fully, our individual power is enfeebled, and we become easily overpowered and overwhelmed by all kinds of influences in our lives.

The power of the breath embraces all and can carry illness, depression, and rage out to others, just as it may carry love, sympathy, and healing when arising from one who is pure in heart. Therefore, we must be vigilant in order to protect ourselves from negative energies, and to send out only healing or positive energy to the world. Breath is the key to our whole energetic process, and is particularly important for full, free, flowing, fluid vocal expression.

The quality of the air we breathe is also very important, so attempt to keep your office or home free from air pollutants. By burning incense you will help to purify the air. My favorite is frankincense, which I have discovered to be a powerful healing essence. This resin or oil cleans both astral and emotional energies from the environment, and so helps to bring about peace and tranquility.

Rhythm

Rhythm is at the heart of the power of breath. The fluid motion of ebb and flow, inflow and outflow, is one of the principle circadian rhythms, and therefore very similar to the movement of the tides, as the individual waves stretch onto the shoreline before once more returning to the body of the ocean. Circadian rhythms are the biorhythms of each twenty-four-hour cycle and can be illustrated by the tidal flow of the oceans, the movement from day into night, the transitions of the seasons, and the migration of animals and birds. Indeed, rhythm is the key to all activity on our planet —the effort/freeness balance of each action, the active/passive force within much of life, the dynamic/stillness flow that is at the core of our changing energies. Therefore, in order to breathe fully and consciously, rhythm must be established. Lack or imbalance of this rhythmic force can be the cause of much imbalance and ill health. Regular and rhythmic conscious breathing gives health to the body and inspiration to the mind.

Relaxation

The only way we can give the best of ourselves is if we are relaxed, and the only way we can fully experience relaxation is if our breath flows freely through our bodies. By the term "relaxation," I do not mean the heavy inertia that often accompanies unconscious "relaxation." To "chill out" often means to simply flop, heavily and without awareness of benefit to the body. The relaxation I believe in is the psycho-physical state of readiness felt when balancing the effort used to achieve action with the freeness used to yield. If we merely engage in effort, or the masculine principle of doing, we often become tense and rigid. Conversely, if we only engage in freeness, or the feminine principle of being, we can easily become inert. However, if we balance both effort and freeness, our energy is more accurately used as we balance the masculine and feminine principles within us, thus creating a true state of rest or relaxation.

The Core Energies

Balance is achieved by allowing space for opposing core energies within us to harmonize. Everything exists in duality and has opposite poles or its masculine and feminine sides. From this principle I have created a list of Universal Core Energies (see below), which I use in my work to help those in need of balance, and which you can use to find balance in yourself and your life. When you feel yourself to be dominated by one of these states, remind yourself of the opposite state and breathe in its energy in order to restore your balance.

UNIVERSAL CORE ENERGIES

Masculine	Feminine
Yang	Yin
Doing	Being
Effort	Freeness
Active	Passive
Dynamic	Stillness
Electric	Magnetic
Thinking	Feeling
Head	Heart/Gut
Intellectuality	Emotionality
Left Brain	Right Brain
Rationality	Sensuality
Positive	Negative
Penetrating	Yielding
Right Body	Left Body
Seen	Hidden
Sound	Silence
Gold	Silver
Sun	Moon

This list could continue into infinity because all things exist with an opposite: there is no such thing as love without hate, fear without freedom, and pain without pleasure.

This is the core essence of The Alchemy of Voice—the understanding that all conditions may be transmuted (moved from one energy into another) once we know the potential ingredients. If I fear "rejection," it is because I believe myself "to be rejectable," and so will create rejection in my life, as thought creates reality. But if I shift my energy and find within myself acceptance, then I am able to achieve a balanced state.

Athletes, in their pursuit of physical excellence, explore profound states of muscle strength, alertness, and freeness. Whatever their skill, whatever their practice, there is always the awareness of the need to balance the zeal to achieve with the patience of letting go. This is a notion that moves them to find a balance where they reach a space of "limitless power." This is when the race runs them rather than they run the race, when they tap into a current of force that allows them to feel a sense of infinite knowledge and understanding. They call this "the zone." If your quest is to climb the mountain of life, literally or metaphorically, do you assault the mountain as you climb, or do you allow the mountain to draw you steadily upward to its peak?

We all experience this in our different ways. For example, if we have worked late into the night for an examination, once the work has been done we let go and trust. When we do this, the answers on the examination paper seem to flow effortlessly—if we are not waiting for failure, that is!

Many actors feel this heightened state of consciousness when they are working, and often describe the sensation as being in complete empathy with the life rhythms of the characters they are portraying; the integration is total—physically, emotionally, mentally, and spiritually.

I once worked with another very sensitive and talented leading actor while he rehearsed *Hamlet.* He was able to move easily into a space of not doing and being, but of existing, like an "isness," where all energies meet a point of stillness. Through doing this, his senses became so heightened that in the moment when Hamlet sees his father's ghost, the actor literally believed he saw the ghost of his own father, who had died some months earlier. If we as actors move our egos aside and simply trust by letting go, we stop playing the character and allow the character to play us. For most of us the idea of "letting go," of "yielding," is a rather alarming notion. Yet once we do, we allow our energies to shift into an opposing state, from negative to positive, and from there into the perfect balance from which all things are possible.

Silence, Solitude, and Stillness

Breathing and relaxation techniques are at the heart of the ability to "let go" and at the heart of all voice work. Silence, Solitude, and Stillness (SSS) is the term I give to the particular breathing/relaxation process at the center of my work; it is an essential prelude to the discovery of your signature note, which will follow in the next chapter.

If you can take just twenty minutes a day to go through this process, your life will become more balanced as you produce calm, commanding, and conscious energies in your life. This will lead you to feel more healthy, wealthy, and wise, whether mentally or physically, materially or spiritually.

My experience has led me to believe that many breathing techniques currently being taught are conflicting and unclear. Since the opening of the "thought corridor" between East and West in the 1950s and 1960s, much information has flooded through, about yoga, acupuncture, transcendental meditation, martial art practices, and many other disciplines. At the core of these processes lies the conviction and consciousness of breath as the force of life itself. The exposure of the Western mind to many different breathing techniques may have led to confusion.

In order to avoid these conflicts I will be precise about what I believe to be the easiest and most accurate process for refined breathing management: a system that opens the finer feelings of the human experience. Before I outline the breathing exercise, however, I want to explain what happens to the brain when we enter a period of deep relaxation through breath.

BRAIN WAVES

Deep breathing affects our entire biochemistry It slows our heart and respiration rate, and we subsequently move into a lower, harmonized brain wave activity known as Alpha. Different brain waves lead to one of four different states of consciousness.

1. Beta Waves – found in the "awake" state of daily consciousness.
2. Alpha Waves – found in the space between sleeping and waking.
3. Theta Waves – found during deep meditation and sleep.
4. Delta Waves – found during deep, deep sleep or coma.

Moving into the Alpha state through deep breathing techniques produces feelings of well-being and peace, which in turn can open a door to creativity, intuition, and a space of limitless possibility.

Many people working in creative fields have discovered that "inspired invention" arises out of, or can accompany, a period of deep relaxation. Einstein is reported to have discovered the Theory of Relativity while sunbathing, and not while standing at a blackboard expostulating complex formulae. In the wonderfully relaxed state that accompanies sunbathing, he imagined the sunbeams, which glinted through his eyelashes, to be fired off into deep outer space. But no matter how he attempted to journey with these transmissions of light, he always found himself returning to the space where he lay. In the Alpha state he used his imagination to attempt an explanation of what was happening. Then he brought his rational thought process to clarify the whole event. The result was an epoch-making scientific formula: $E=MC^2$. This discovery shocked the principles of established science and significantly led Einstein to say, "imagination is more important than knowledge."

Alpha waves alter human consciousness to such an extent that the right and left hemispheres of the brain connect. This was discovered in 1981 as the result of the extraordinary collaborative effort of two scientists at the University of California. After twenty years of research, Robert Ornstein and Roger Sperry won the Nobel Prize for their ground-breaking research, which established that the neocortex of the brain functions bilaterally, each part being responsible for different actions.

The left, rational side of the brain is responsible for:

> cognition
> words
> numbers
> analysis
> logic
> lists.

The right, imaginative side of the brain is responsible for:

> intuition
> color
> imagination
> dimension
> rhythm
> music.

Einstein's discovery was a wonderful example of right-brain (imagination) firing a response in the left-brain (reason) so that both hemispheres colluded to create a fuller understanding.

The paradigm of the brain's hemispheres evokes an even greater question about our preparation for internal and external balance, particularly with regard to established educational practice and its emphasis on the development of logical, left-brain usage. Conversely, through Silence, Solitude, and Stillness, we may acquire many skills to assist "centeredness" and balance in our lives, thus counteracting the unilateral, fixed systems that so many of us are used to.

The Anatomy of Breathing

It is most important to understand that beyond our lungs deflating and inflating, there are two parts of the body that regulate the external muscular activity of breath: the ribcage and the abdomen. This is particularly salient to remember as, today, much attention is applied to the abdomen only. Many teachers of breathing techniques suggest that we should "feel the diaphragm moving into the pelvic floor." This is a biological impossibility; however, one *can* feel the movement of the upper abdominal wall in relation to the breath's entry. This occurs when the internal muscle of the diaphragm spontaneously moves downward, affecting the stomach's contents, and, therefore, allowing the movement of the belly outward. However, if this occurs singularly, the movement of the ribcage is negated, starving the upper, internal lung area of oxygen.

I believe this confusion has arisen from the experience of deep-rest breathing rhythm techniques, which require minimal muscular activity in the torso and can be felt predominantly in the abdomen. However, in order to gain a fully oxygenated body for maximum expression, we must feel the entire mechanism of both ribcage and abdomen opened by the action of breath.

So many of the vocal casualties I come across in my work create their voice dysfunction by breathing into the stomach alone, which produces severe internal pressure. This is particularly so for those who use their voice professionally, who require a strong, robust breathing support to maintain and open a strong, athletic vocal position and resonance.

Some time ago, I coached a leading opera singer who experienced tremendous tension in his torso and upper abdomen, accompanied by dizziness and heart palpitations. In order to support the tremendous vigor of Wagner's music, this singer was pushing down into his diaphragm and creating pressure within his heart's pulmonary musculature. He was extremely unwell, and I felt great sympathy for him, although I experienced some surprise as he demonstrated the abdominal distension occurring as he attempted to push breath into his belly. His dilemma was soon corrected when I suggested that opening the rib swing, particularly through the back "floating ribs," would ease the diaphragm movement. As soon as he adopted this technique his health problems disappeared, and he went on to effortlessly produce an enormously strong sound and to sing Wagner's challenging music.

The Breathing Exercise

Here is the easy, step-by-step SSS breathing practice (Silence, Solitude and Stillness) that I have found to be most effective.

1. First, check that you have space for Silence, Solitude, and Stillness, meaning that you will not be disturbed by anything or anybody. Switch off any disturbing electrical equipment, and make sure your voicemail is on! Remove your shoes, too.
2. Lie down on your back, with your head supported by a small cushion and your spine as aligned as possible.
3. Bend your knees toward the ceiling, drawing your feet along the floor, and keeping your heels in close connection with your bottom. Make sure your feet are eight to ten inches apart, so as not to tense your thighs, groin, or lower abdomen. This will allow you to feel your legs supporting themselves.
4. Feel the whole of your back against the floor. It is important to check that the lumbar or small of your back is as flat as possible, but do not use pressure to flatten your body. If you need to, put your feet onto a chair, and the whole of your back will then feel long and wide and spread.
5. Place your open palms on the base of your ribcage, with your elbows resting comfortably on the floor each side of your body. Let the length and breadth of your back relax and open and try not to cross your fingers—just keep your hands open against your body, then the energy will flow rather than being closed and tense.
6. Make sure you feel gravity, letting your body spread on the floor surface.
7. Imagine a laser beam of light shining down into the floor from the base of your spine. Follow its journey down through the various strata: the earth's crust, the soil, the clay, and stone, into bedrock.
    This is a visualization of the force of gravity in your body; feel its arrival in Mother Earth as being magnetic. Allow the laser to once more travel up into your body and feel the whole of your being releasing into this feeling of weight and gravity—your back long and wide, each muscle responding to this wonderful openness. Weight means relaxed freeness. Lightness means tension, the opposite of relaxed.
8. Breathe all the breath out through parted lips, wait a moment,

and then feel the need to breathe in. Breathe in, feeling the unseen air as a color or light moving down your spine, like an elevator moving down its shaft. Concentrate on the air expanding the base of your ribs, so that you feel a widening, particularly in your back, through the floating ribs. Relax your shoulders if you feel them tense. Then breathe out all the air through your lips. Do not push, just support the breath, otherwise you will feel your throat close.

9. When you feel the need to breathe in, allow the air to widen the base of your ribs once more, making sure the upper chest and shoulder area is completely free. Breathing in through your nostrils and out through your lips will stimulate the intake. Again, if you see the breath as colored *chi* moving down your spine, it will help you to open up.

10. This time, checking your throat is free, whisper the breath out to a count of ten, feeling the muscles between each rib supporting the effort. Relax the shoulders and don't worry if your throat closes; the stronger and more aware your rib muscles become, the easier it will be to release the glottal pressure in your throat.

11. After a complete out-breath, wait until you feel the need to breathe in, and then repeat the same procedure, feeling your ribs widen, particularly through the back rib swing.

12. Check that your upper spine, neck, and shoulders are completely free. Keep practicing this breathing, increasing the count to fifteen and then twenty. If you wish, sound each out-breath as *sssssss*. On each recovery wait a second or two until you feel the need to breathe, so that you don't push. Your ribs will open of their own volition, so wait to feel the muscles spring open as the ribs expand.

This completes the first stage; take a rest from "doing," that is, from the effort of action, for a few minutes. I hope you will have felt the ribcage expansion that is so important and a freeing in the upper chest, shoulders, and neck.

In the second stage it is important to feel the same action, but this time to take the breath into your body's interior, wide and then deep; feel yourself just "being" this. When the movement of the ribs opens the diaphragm, you will feel the upper abdominal wall shift outward. This is called "rooting down."

13. Check again the feeling of length and width in your back, with the weight of your body resting easily on the floor, a balance between doing and being.

14. Breathe all the breath out, and then wait to feel the need to breathe in. Breathe in, letting your ribs widen, like a rubber tire, all the way around your torso. With a hand on your upper abdomen, feel the outward movement of your stomach. Try not to push and feel the breath touching down, deep inside.

15. As you let the breath release, focus it into the vowel sound *haw*. Feel the sound coming from the center of your body, from the earth of your core, rooted and full of your body's weight. You will feel the vibration of resonance throughout your whole being. If you only feel the sound in your head this means your throat is tense. Try to simulate a yawn; this will open your throat and release the metallic or nasal aspects of the sound.

16. Repeat the in-breath and make the following sounds, feeling each sound as you make it:
     Haw. Sense the vibration in your solar plexus.
     It is the *Earth* element.
     Hoo. Sense the vibration in your heart center.
     It is the *Water* element.
     How. Sense the vibration in your throat center.
     It is the *Air* element.
     Hee. Sense the vibration in your head center.
     It is the *Fire* element.
     zzzzzzz. Feel the vibration through the whole of your spine.

17. Stop for a moment, letting your body breathe for itself. Listen in to a distant sound—real or imaginary—switching off any "mind-chatter." Feel the dynamic stillness. The stillness will wave or spiral through your body, and the subtle, dynamic breath rhythm will occur in your stomach. Connect with all your senses, one at a time, and feel the quality of inner connectedness and outer presence. You will feel a wonderful sense of inner richness and detachment from the outer world. This is your inner truth ready for outer expression.

Repeat this breathing exercise once or twice every day, and feel the mental, physical, emotional, and spiritual enhancement as you use your breath to nourish and uplift yourself.

Physicality: the Architecture of the Body

Just as the superstructure of a great building supports the infrastructure of the life that takes place within it, so our bodies need to be able to support us, with the spine as the superstructure, supporting the movement of muscles and joints. When you are able to achieve an open, free physicality you will feel a sense of personal power exude from your body, so much so that others will notice and comment on this. You will also be able to achieve a full, flexible breath that supports the openness of your voice.

To achieve this open and free physical state it is necessary to pay attention to the way you use your body and hold yourself. By doing this, and by strengthening and supporting your body, you will discover what is most noble about your body and, indeed, your life.

Hamlet provides us with eloquent advice about the power of our bodies: "What a piece of work is a man, how noble in reason, how infinite in faculties, in form and moving how express and admirable, in action how like an Angel, in apprehension how like a God: the beauty of the world, the paragon of animals."

This is a useful model to use to understand more about the amazing nature of our bodies in relation to others and to the world, and to discover how best to create meaningful relationships through "noble," or magnanimous, thoughts and feelings. Creating relationships is at the core of our speaking and our communication with the world; what better way to develop this than through grace and admiration—like an angel.

During the Elizabethan period, a belief was held that man/woman was the microcosm of the macrocosm, and, therefore, the foremost creation of God. In medieval philosophy, it was believed that we were made from a confluence of all the elements: Earth, Water, Air, Fire, and Ether, or the breath of God, the animating principle of the universe. We are made of bones, ligaments, and tendons positioned in elastic suits of muscle. We are blood, sweat, tears, and the electricity of our nerves. I believe our bodies are founded on these principles:

Physical body	–	Earth
Emotional body	–	Water
Mental body	–	Air
Spiritual body	–	Fire

In the earlier SSS exercise we used the vowel sounds *Haw, Hoo, How, Hee*, which correspond with the four elements thus:

Haw – Physical – Earth
Hoo – Emotion – Water
How – Mental – Air
Hee – Spirit – Fire

Later, we will tune these elemental sounds and energies from your signature note into the sound of intention. But first you need to organize the frame of your body, so that your spine may fully operate as the conduit or conductor of force that it truly is. Try the following spinal alignment exercise, and include it with the breathing exercise as part of your daily routine.

ALIGNING YOUR BODY

1. Check you have space in which to stand comfortably, then place your feet in a parallel position, about six or eight inches apart. If you feel that the parallel feet position draws your knees together, open your toes slightly. However, make sure your feet are not too wide apart or too turned out, as this will rotate your hips and push your pelvis forward.

2. Rock backward and forward over the heels and toes of your feet until you reach a comfortable position balanced through each foot between heel and toe, and through your insteps. This will feel slightly strange if you are used to standing with your weight over your heels—a common habit. When we move forward in life from the latter position, we move forward with our weight backward, which is very retroactive. In other words, we carry the unresolved nature of ourselves (our baggage and unexpressed feelings) into the future.

3. Try walking around, feeling how freeing it is to carry your weight forward. But do check that you do not look like the leaning tower of Pisa; use a full-length mirror to help you see your physical alignment.

4. Check that your knees are not braced back, with your thighs and calves tensed. This is something we often do when we are nervous or anxious, rather like gripping onto the floor. Indeed, this tension is often accompanied by the toes clawing into the shoes or floor, as if holding on for dear life. Just let go and relax. Our knees are powerfully important movement terminals in our bodies. Through our knees flows our yielding force (imagine someone kneeling in supplication), as well as the pliability to achieve complex movements, when the knees become shock absorbers.

5. Check that your pelvis, the moving center of your physicality, is "tucked under" without clenching your buttocks, knees, or thighs. Simply place the backs of your hands on the lower spine (your lumbar region) and caress your hands downward, tucking or tilting your pelvis under slightly to lengthen the lower spine. Many of us are very arched in this area, which shortens the lower back and tightens the muscles.

6. Now feel the length of your spine lifting up from the base. Feel your lumbar area open, your middle back area lengthen, your upper spine long, right into the full length of your neck. Finally, check the position of your head, lengthen your neck vertebrae, but don't push your chin forward.

7. Check that you are not standing round-shouldered or bracing your shoulders back. If you feel the need to, as you lengthen your spine, bring your hands to chest height, opening your elbows outward. This will allow you to feel open, rather than constricted through the heart-center area.

8. If you can, look at yourself in profile in a mirror. You will see your shoulders balanced over your hips and your hips over the center of your feet; this is classical physical alignment.

9. Take a deep breath in, widening rather than lifting the breath into your body. See the breath as light filling the whole of your physical form, as your body may be seen as the "architecture" of your being. This will make you feel long and wide and strong.

10. Sound *Haa* right through the center of your body. Imagine there are lips in the center of your chest; this will help you focus the whole of your energy into the complete sound—*your* sound.

This spinal alignment, feeling through the whole of your body's architecture, is often difficult to achieve alone, so work with a partner or friend, if possible. What you will feel is a greater sense of breath management and support. In turn, this will allow you to feel vital and full of potency, which will inevitably be communicated to those around you.

In Conclusion…

Breath is our vitality and life force. Allowing the full, free flow of your breath through your body will energize, restore, and invigorate you. Make your breathing practice an essential part of each day, for through this breathing practice you are laying the groundwork for the most important step of all—the discovery of your personal signature note. As you repeat and enjoy the breathing exercises, you will feel the petty things of daily life dissolved by the sanctity of breath. With this release from disturbance you will feel the revelation that it is easy to open your heart, and access the power of your innate wisdom.

CHAPTER 4

Your Signature Note

*It is the state of vibration to which a person is tuned
that accounts for his soul's note.*
—HAZRAT INAYAT KHAN

We are all unique, and particularly we each have our own note, our own vibration. This is the "signature sound" of our being: individual, distinctive, and unlike that of any other person. It is the sound that sits at the core of our physical body and, therefore, reflects who we truly and completely are.

Once you have experienced your signature note, you will feel a strong sense of "re-cognition" and of the "lightness" of the sound you are making. It is like coming home to the wholeness of who you are, and will open you to far greater personal power and the ability to transform all areas of your life. Discovering our signature note opens our vocal potential, and with it our whole being, moving us away from the fears that lead us to limiting our voices by trapping them in our heads.

In this chapter, I will explain why I believe our signature sound is stored deep within the cells of our bodies, and I will lead you, step by step, toward the discovery of your own signature note. I will then take you on to discover ways of using your signature note by focusing your sound energy in four major energy centers, or chambers of your body.

Fear and Tension

Often when we experience the pressures of life, we become fearful and move away from the core of our being. Feeling takes us into areas of our existence that we have perhaps not fully come to terms with, particularly when they relate to our earlier lives as children. These sensitivities can be very painful, and because we find it hard to manage the power of the feeling, we "pack" it away somewhere in our bodies. In other words, when we do not want to feel or to let others feel the enormity of something that once made us feel out of control or full of panic, we create a great deal of physical and emotional tension within our bodies. The result is that we "store" our voice in our head, particularly by clenching the jaw and lifting the back of the tongue through tension and, therefore, closing the throat. This prevents sound from resonating through the whole of our body—we literally become a "talking head." You can repeat the exercise from page 38 to experience this tension—make the sound "*GEE, GEE, GEE*" with a tight and then a relaxed tongue to feel the difference.

The exercise on page 38 clearly illustrates how we close or trap our voice in our head in order to move away from deep feelings, or to avoid feeling out of control. One difficulty that arises from this is that making sound in the head can feel very controlled, because we are so used to controlling our lives with the product of our head: our thoughts. We may find this sense of control reassuring, but what others perceive when we operate thus is quite different; they feel uncomfortable and uncontrolled themselves, because we are not sharing ourselves fully Often the same tension happens in others as we speak, and they also unconsciously close their throat and trap their sound in their head.

The next time you are listening to a major news broadcast about an atrocity in the world, notice where you feel the information in your body. Broadcasters present literal, objective information about the event, and often use a cerebral voice by closing their throats, so as not to feel. Observe what is happening in your throat, and how you hold your breath while listening to such distressing information.

Discovering your signature note will allow you to release feelings that may have been "packed away," and to sound your voice through the whole of your being, so that it rings true and authentic and is ultimately powerful.

Cellular Memory

Many people believe, at first, that their signature note is inaccessible, and that discovering it will, therefore, be impossible. I believe that anyone can access their signature note. We have simply "unremembered" our primal note—a sound that was largely kept alive through expressing the oral traditions of our cultures. This vibration is stored deep within our archetypal consciousness, which is derived from the collective unconscious. We have "unremembered" it as a result of the emphasis we place on the purely cerebral action of our lives and the intellectual drive to keep "doing" life, to the point where we are fixated on the "ends to be gained" rather than the "means whereby we create our potential."

This primal sound is stored within our cellular memory, waiting for us to fulfil its promise by discovering our truth in our signature note, and, therefore, a sincere, authentic voice.

There is now clear scientific evidence to suggest that we store memories not just in our brain but in the cells of our bodies. The eminent biologist Rupert Sheldrake enlarged our view of the way we learn and use memory by developing the theory of cellular memory. He says, "Living organisms not only inherit genes, but also morphic fields. Genes are passed on materially from ancestors and enable them to make particular kinds of protein molecules; the morphic fields are inherited non-materially by resonance, not just from direct ancestors but from other members of the species. The developing organism tunes into the morphic field of its species, and thus draws upon a pooled, or collective, 'cellular memory.'" In other words, we pass on to our children not only our genes but the collective memories of our ancestors.

This theory also mirrors the view of the psychoanalyst Carl Jung, who suggested that there exists a "collective unconscious," an inherited collective memory that underpins the whole substance of human consciousness.

These attitudes are in direct opposition to the mechanistic theories of evolution developed by scientists during the seventeenth century, the most common of which suggested that memory depends on material "memory traces" that are stored within our brains and have no connection with anyone or anything else.

Everything I have discovered about the human voice and the power of our individual sound-making leads me to believe that we do indeed have cellular memory in which is stored the original sound of our species—"the song of our soul," if you like. What is more, the information stored in our cellular memory is accessible; through the use of specific vocal exercises, we can recover these memories and use them to empower ourselves, here and now.

This opens the wondrous possibility of rediscovering the ability to make sound that comes from the core of our being and that is wholly true to who we are. When this occurs, the fullness, resonance, poetry, soulfulness, and range of the voice is greatly opened, as is the ability to express feelings freely. With the free flow of energy that results, we reestablish the opportunity to communicate with integrity. We will be heard more easily and will communicate with everyone at a far deeper and more profound level, and so draw people to us magnetically. Those around us will automatically respond to us differently, sensing our authenticity, our power, and our wholeheartedness.

Perpetual Movement

Human beings are not alone in producing a signature note. Every solid form existing in our three-dimensional world has its own specific and distinctive note, or vibration, which in turn creates its own resonance and frequency. Everything—a tree, a table, a glass, or indeed a human body—is in a state of perpetual movement. The matter we perceive as solid is merely a cloak for energy.

All matter is made up of atoms, in which electrons spin around the nucleus, producing vibrations from movement. When vibration occurs, a sound is emitted, which travels in the form of a wave. This happens at varying speeds. Electrons that spin fast produce a high note, while those that spin slowly produce a low note. These speeding sounds are measured by units referred to as hertz (cycles per second).

The vibration of any object also creates a resonance frequency. Imagine striking a note on a piano. One hears the pitch of the note, and then the resonance produced by other notes tuned to the same frequency. This resonance is like an echo effect, created as the sound waves oscillate through the disturbed air. When other notes sound it means they are in synergy with the initial note; these sounds are referred to as harmonics.

In the same way, we can find the sound of our own note. Just as the resonance of the other piano notes echo the note played, we can "play" or vocalize a note that echoes all of our constituent parts and, therefore, becomes a reflection of our whole physical self. This note is our signature note.

Finding Your Note

Imagine that your entire vocal range is stretched horizontally, like the keyboard of a piano. The middle of the piano's keyboard is marked by the note "middle C." The bass notes, below middle C, are the low notes and the treble notes, above middle C, are the high notes.

The notes on the piano are grouped into octaves. The word "octave" arises from the Latin for "eight" and refers to the eight-note sequence on which the whole of Western classical music is based, otherwise known as the diatonic scale: CDEFGABC.

If you were to play the treble notes in the higher octave of the piano, you would hear high pitches. Similarly, if one were to produce high notes with the voice, the resonance would be predominantly in the upper body or head. Conversely, if one plays only bass notes on the piano, one would need to strike the keys in the lower octaves. If we relate this to the voice producing only bass notes, the sound would arise from the lower part of the body, the stomach and pelvic area. However, if we imagine two hands playing the piano keys astride treble and bass, one would experience a harmony of sound, reflecting the potential range of the instrument. If we relate this to our voice, all we need do is convert the horizontal plane of the keyboard into a vertical line, and if we imagine this within our spine, we can feel a range of sound is opened within our body.

Our spine is the major conduit for the energy within our body. It is the neural channel transmitting information to every cell we possess, which can happen in less than twenty milliseconds. One brain cell's reaction can spread to hundreds of thousands of cells in a time span that is about ten times shorter than it takes for an eye to blink. This is the most specific reason why healthy positioning of our spine is essential for full and fluid use of our bodies. If we imagine our voice in the center of the spine, around the upper abdomen or heart area, the spine will vibrate the center note or signature sound of our whole range.

Try sounding the note *Hum* into your forehead after taking a full breath, supported and sustained. Try not to sing, but sound a sustained *Hum* at the top of your speaking range. Feel the sound in your forehead, at a point just above your eyes. Then slide the *Hum* down the entire length of your spine—you will probably cover two, maybe three octaves of sound (this varies from person to person). Complete the exercise at the lowest note you are easily capable of sounding, deep down in the base of your spine or in the pit of your stomach. Do not push and tighten your throat: the slide should be easy and flow freely.

This exercise can be very enjoyable—it's fun to feel the tickling resonance zooming down your spine. Use the visual image of an elevator moving down its shaft to help you; see it as color, like the light-force energy of your breath awakening the sound. If it is difficult to see a color, imagine that you are seeing it as white light.

Keep practicing this until you feel comfortable with the skill. Then try directing the *Hum* to a point just into the lower part of your sternum. It is important to keep breathing freely and expanding the physical flexibility of the sound. When you have ridden the sound from forehead to sternum you will feel your whole body full of resonance. When you reach your breastbone, imagine there are lips appearing from your chest, or a beam of light emerging from the center of your heart area. Then open the *Hum* into *Hah* (the heart vowel, see page 88) and you will feel your note. The sound will feel as though it arises from the center of your spine, spreading through your entire being. Again, this is rather like dropping a stone into the middle of a still pond and watching the ripples move to the edge of the pond.

With a little practice you will feel the whole resonance of your voice arriving from this center. The upper and lower resonance, or harmonic, of your voice will come together to a point of clarity, and so you will feel the significance of your entire physical being sounding its signature note.

Keep practicing this simple sequence and, as repetition is the mother of skill, you will eventually feel the sound to be distinctly true and whole and will be able to trust it. When this happens, blend the *Hum* into *Hah,* and then into a spoken count, from one to five. When you do this, you will feel the core power of your being arising in the note and resonance. You will feel a sense of sitting in the middle of yourself.

Add to it an affirmation of your choice, or a line of verse such as "Tiger, tiger burning bright, in the forest of the night," and while the sound of your note is still fresh, answer the following questions:

What color is the sound?
Which word most specifically conveys the feeling and power of the sound to you?
Which image immediately comes to mind that clearly evokes the purity of this power?
Which sound most represents its essence?

Noting and remembering the answers that come to you will help you to recall and repeat your signature note more easily in the future, as words and images anchor us.

Elizabeth's story is a wonderful example of what it means to discover your signature note. A strong, innovative personality who had proved herself effective as a manager in several high-caliber jobs over a period of about fifteen years, Elizabeth was hugely successful in her working life. A few months before we met she had been head-hunted and offered the job of Head of Human Resources with a major international company.

Elizabeth accepted the job, but sadly her life partner of ten years could not cope with the status change created by her new job, and after a period of breakdown he left her. She immediately became ill and lost her voice. Toward the end of her recovery she came to see me.

Elizabeth was very tense, a result of the period of emotional difficulty she had just been through with her estranged partner and the new challenge of heading a department that employed thousands of people. Could she do it?

Her past experience proved her ability. But Elizabeth felt no power in her voice and with the possibility of high-profile meetings and presentations to give, she simply felt terrified.

I immediately introduced her to the notion of her signature note and the authentic power that it would generate. She was fascinated. We approached breathing exercises for relaxation, stamina, and power, after which I took her through the "Sound and Body Centring Sequence," otherwise known as the Silence, Solitude, and Stillness phase, outlined in Chapter 3. This sequence is the core focus for discovering one's note and the route to sound healing.

Elizabeth was determined and worked hard to free her throat through sighing and yawning releases, so that we easily found her note. As soon as she felt the note resonate she began to cry tears of joy. She said that she felt years of tension release or lift from her chest and upper spine. Images of her father also came to her mind, a man who was deeply loving but always tried to keep her and her three sisters "in place." "I believe he was frightened of female power," she told me.

Over three or four sessions, we tuned her awareness to the newfound power of her note, and related it to the presentations she gave at work. These were proving more and more effortless, largely as a consequence of the increased confidence and inner power she felt. She reported that she had only felt this degree of independence, authenticity, and joy once in her earlier life—when she won a scholarship to university.

We still see each other once in a while, when Elizabeth wishes to consult me for "fine tuning." Her career has gone from strength to strength, and she has found a new love, with whom she is deeply happy.

The Dynamic Energy of the Voice

Finding your signature note, or the sound of your truth, will startle your heart into its own awakening. From this, you will be able to develop ways of truly defining sound energy; that is, centering your voice in four key physical energy centers within your body, so that your signature note can be more fully used. In this way, you will be able to focus different aspects of your being through sound. Using "sound intention" creates extremely powerful effects—sound crystallizes intention. Whichever physical center you are sounding in, the intention behind it should always be coming from your note, or the heart, the illumined center of your existence.

These energy centers hold thoughts and feelings directly connected with sense memories and can, therefore, provide us with a way to release long-held feelings, as well as to discover a more detailed and profound sensory experience in every aspect of our lives.

THE HEAD CENTER

Sound a note on the vowel *EE* on a fully supported breath, centering it in your forehead. Think of the resonance as white or pink. Your whole head will be filled with the high energy of sound. Now try a line of verse, such as: "Thus with imagined wing our swift scene flies." Make sure you are not cutting off sound solely in your head. Do this by making sure your throat and jaw are free, so that a connection with your note or heart center is still there. Try saying *Ga Ga Ga*, tight and then free. Do it several times, and you will notice that this is achieved by lifting or dropping the back of your tongue against the soft palate, which is the soft muscle at the rear of the roof of your mouth. You can feel whether you are closing the sound through too much effort by tightening the tongue too much, or keeping the tone open in your throat by using the tongue more freely. The tongue and throat act like a valve; the energy in this area either opens or closes the flow of tone through the "resonance chamber" of the whole body.

This kind of objective sound occurs when we are engaged in exchanging thoughts that are basically informative or intellectual. After years of using this exercise with actors, politicians, and captains of industry, a general guideline has emerged: that the tone of this head center may be called *I INFORM*. The energy is electrical, like bright white light, and in nature feels full of fire.

Brilliant high-energy comedy is focused through the head center, particularly when the comedian is using wit. Wit arises from a cerebral play of words as a commentary on life. It is not so much a belly-laugh, more a wonderfully articulated, cut-glass explosion of thought. If full feeling were engaged instead, the energy would take on a weight, or gravitas, that would alter its transmission.

I remember working with one of the United Kingdom's leading comediennes, a woman who had her own very successful TV show but wanted to discover a way of making more of an impact with her voice. We moved the jokes around through this vibration of sound, and she felt that they had a brilliance more spectacular than before. Her television producer confided in me that while he'd always felt there was an even greater potential in her, he had never felt her full power until this time; it was as though her comedy timing had become underpinned by a greater fluency, but one that was also very specific in tempo. The producer felt she had become even more deft in using her voice to focus the listener.

Try telling jokes or humorous stories to your family and friends and see the effect you have on their listening.

THE THROAT CENTER

Sound a note on the vowel *OW* on a fully supported breath, simply in your throat. Make sure your breath is still full and free, while imagining the color light blue, which will help to open the energy of the resonance. You will notice a completely different feeling from the head energy, arising from the energy of the sound. Experience has led me to think of this center as *I Soothe*.

If this is difficult to achieve, try simulating a yawn or a sigh on the note *OW*. Imagine your favorite drink sliding easily down your throat, and notice the difference. Visualizing sensory stimuli always helps us to open a sensual response, particularly in our voice.

Now try a line of verse, such as "The Barge she sat in like a burnished throne, burned on the water." You will feel the sound to be very softly sensual if you open the vowels.

Whenever we are engaged in seductive lovemaking, wooing, or singing a lullaby, we focus most of our energy into our throats. Surprisingly, political persuasion can also arise from the throat center. This center is soft, easy, and soothing by nature, often inducing Alpha brain rhythms in the listener. So if you are attempting to relax someone, think light blue and center your sound in this way. Your listener will virtually fall into your arms!

Some time ago, I was running an "Alchemy of Voice" workshop in the United States. Some of the leading psychotherapists in the country were present, and one man from Chicago asked me, in a very gruff tone, if I could corroborate my findings. I took this gentleman through a brief relaxation process and asked him to feel a sense of Air, or *I Soothe,* in his throat, like maple syrup or honey. He then spoke a few lines of a William Blake poem, and the ladies gasped at the power and beauty of the tone. The gruffness had left him, the sincerity was palpable, and indeed one of the ladies was so affected that they started dating immediately after the weekend workshop had finished. Both of them had been alone and single for some years, so I was delighted when six months later I had the joy of being invited to read a prayer at their marriage ceremony.

THE HEART CENTER

We are back to the heart center, with which we always connect our voice when we wish to feel truly open and a sense of our own power.

Take a deep breath, full and open, and sound *OO*, imagining the color green through the lip image in the center of your chest (see page 65). The resonance will be much deeper and less brilliant than in the head center. There will be a feeling of *gravitas*, or weight, maybe even a sense of solemnity. Whatever the feeling, sense how your heart opens to its richness and full glory, providing you with strength and courage and sovereignty.

Now try a line of verse, such as "Brave warriors Clifford and Northumberland, come make him stand on this molehill here."

This sound is so often taken from us by powerful people in our lives, when they become daunted by the possibility that our power may be as great as theirs. If they are very controlling, they may feel threatened by the potential of others and, therefore, attempt to manipulate them into weaker positions. Others can only take your power if you allow them to. Centering your sound in the heart returns your power to you; after all, the heart is the organ of truth, the center of all authentic feeling, so what more powerful energy could there be?

This exercise often brings up wonderfully mixed emotions in those who try it and who have previously denied themselves the joy of using its power.

I was once consulted by a leading politician, Mr G, who was due to give a major speech at a rally. He felt diminished in status as a result of the failure of a bill debate in the Houses of Parliament, which had been his particular project. On meeting it was obvious that this kind man had lost all connection with his archetypal kingship and feeling of personal power.

I introduced Mr G to the notion of this energy center and how it was very waterlike in texture, being so close to the emotional center of the heart. We decided to call the center *I EMPOWER*, as it represents the true power of personal sovereignty.

Mr G was creative in his thought process and very open to new ideas, and our time together was easy and free-flowing. He started using the energy of this center and quickly rediscovered his personal power by seeing and hearing the effect it had on colleagues. This led to a successful and moving speech in the Commons and a highly effective speech at his constituency rally, where a noisy faction in the audience was easily won over by the power of his tone and rhetoric. Winston Churchill often sounded from this position of power during his major speeches of the Second World War.

THE PELVIC CENTER

Breathe in wide and deep and sound *AW* on the lowest comfortable note you can sound. Imagine red-brown earth deep in the base of your spine, the pit of your stomach or general pelvic area. The immediate sound feeling will be one that folds the earthy core of you into itself. The feeling is very impressive, creating an indentation or impact within the very substance of you. This is a sound we rarely make, except when we are moved beyond all rationality into the deep Earth Mother core of our experience.

This sound is rarely expressive, meaning that we primarily use it for the transmission of womb-oriented feelings; therefore, the sounds we make from here are often not easily verbalized.

Now try a line of verse, such as "O! that this too too solid flesh should melt, thaw and resolve itself into a dew."

I believe we return to this sound when in deep grief or sorrow. For this reason, if you are harboring unexpressed feelings from the past, making this sound may not be a very comfortable experience. However, if you can persist in expressing the sound the feelings will free you for ever from the burden stored deep in your gut.

Quite recently I met a woman who had been referred to me by her holistic doctor. Penny had been through a period of bereavement and was deeply mourning her husband. Complications had arisen, and she had experienced a prolapsed womb and had had to undergo major surgery.

Penny felt crushed. While all this was going on, she developed a feeling of supreme tightness and dryness in her throat and sounded as if she were sitting on her voice. When I heard her, I knew immediately that something deep had not been expressed.

She had held the tragedy of her husband's death in her throat while she led the family and supported her two adult children in their pain. Because of this she had never expressed her own deep feeling of utter loss.

Penny needed to open her Earth energy through the *I MOURN* pelvic energy center. We sounded the *HAW*, but again she could only produce a thin, tight sound that was seemingly caught in her throat. I needed something more, and so while we worked I played sacred songs by a Russian male voice choir— voices that have such depth you can feel the vibrations deep in your stomach. After this I sounded *Haw* into Penny's stomach area, and at last she began to weep, deeply and for some time. We had unplugged years of sorrow, not simply for the loss of her own husband but for other "holdings" of sorrow that she had not expressed, as a consequence of not wanting to trouble anyone. A few hours after this process, all symptoms of throat tightness and dryness left her and she could sound the *HAW* Earth sound with ease and a certain flourish. Penny is now training as a bereavement counselor.

Practice all four of these sound energies to discover the full extent of the possibilities your signature note opens up for you. You will open a greater vocal range; express yourself with greater clarity, openness, and depth; and begin to feel a wonderful sense of personal power, which will enable you to make transformative changes in and to your life. Notice the effect your voice has on other people. Be prepared for people to really notice you—you may feel honored for the first time in a long while.

In Conclusion…

Our voice is the window to our soul. It illustrates or clarifies the whole of our being, a being that vibrates through the wholeness of us—physically, emotionally, mentally, and spiritually. Exploring the potential of sound through the discovery of our signature note and our ability to sound through the body centers may lead us to express feelings that have been held in check for some time. Do not worry about what may come up. Feeling is the language of the soul, so work through the process, remembering that you are always in charge. Allow your signature note to emerge, freeing your feelings, opening your soul, and empowering you. Another great boon will be an increased sensing of other people's voices; eventually, you will be able to read other people's psychological blueprint, just by the way they produce their voice.

CHAPTER 5

CHAKRAS AND THE AURA

The Chakras are similar to electrical batteries:
when tuned they provide dynamic force and qualitative energy.
By the startling of theirenergies they fuse personal liberation,
mundane becomes divine!

—*DJWHAL KHUL THROUGH ALICE BAILEY*

Fresh from the wonderful discovery of your signature note, I want to take you on an exploration of the energy centers of the body known as the chakras, and the subtle, electromagnetic field that surrounds each of us, known as the radiant aura. Once you are familiar with the chakras and are able to harness the pure power of your voice, you will connect with the possibility of healing through sound the imbalances within the body and the body's energy field, clearing illness, unhappiness, and disease.

In this chapter, I will explain the functioning of the body's electromagnetic field through the chakras. These are the databases, or biocomputers, for the energy of our whole being. The physical, emotional, mental, and spiritual bodies merge through the energy of the chakras, and in turn create a field of energy that is the light of the aura.

In order to "see" an aura clearly, an elevation of consciousness is needed as the vibration is of a higher frequency than we normally inhabit. In early Renaissance paintings it is often depicted as the halo over religious or spiritual figures. Most of us cannot see auras because we live lives that make us imbalanced and full of stress, which creates disharmony in our bodies in the form of toxicity.

Fear and worry create excess adrenaline, which diminishes the capability of the T-cells that protect our immune system. This is one of the major reasons for the countless minor ailments that we experience in periods of stress. In addition, the unhealthy foods we eat, the caffeine we drink, our fear of being alone, and our lack of belief in the sacred or spiritual aspects of our lives all diminish our energy field, making the organic matter of our body dense and compact as opposed to light and free.

However, even if we cannot see auras we can still "sense" or apprehend the quality of the aura's force around someone or within an environment. We often say of someone who has great presence or is illuminated, serene, and radiant that they have aura, magnetism, star quality, or are charismatic. In effect what we are sensing is their energy field, their aura, and in this case one that resonates a pure state of mind and body. Conversely, there are those people whom we meet who are really draining; their energy fields are often filled with dark colors and impurities, as a consequence of negative thoughts and feelings.

The aura, or energy field, is created by the light emanations of the chakras, which each have a color. Each chakra also has a specific area of influence within and without our auric being. With practice, the balanced or imbalanced currents of our energy field can be felt and seen in the light energy of the aura. Once imbalances are identified, simple and yet wonderfully effective sound healing exercises can be used to restore wellbeing.

This is very similar to the healing discipline of reiki. Reiki is a Japanese word, of which *rei* means "universe" and *ki* means "force." We live in a universe that is nourished at core by the light of the sun, and so we all channel reiki through our fields. If we are conscious of this process and energy we may empower ourselves when we feel unhappy, weak, or lacking in self-confidence. Similarly, we can be a conduit for other people and help them heal by channeling reiki through ourself; healing means moving back to wholeness.

A simple illustration of how "enlightened" we may feel, having tuned into the reiki force, is the way many of us find ourselves drawn to the countryside, which is less electrically polluted than cities and towns. The natural phenomenon of our plant life feeds us, inspires us and spiritually benefits us.

The Chakras

Within the subtle electromagnetic energy of the body are the seven chakras. The word *chakra* is from the ancient Indian language of Sanskrit, meaning "spinning wheel" or "wheel of light." The chakras form themselves along the conduit of our spine and are centers of force.

Esoteric wisdom reveals that there are twelve chakras within the energy field of the body, seven within and five without. Our focus will be on the seven inner chakras. Each of these has its own specific purpose and vibrates as colored light within the aura of each individual. The aura can be photographed using a technique known as Kirlian photography and is an electromagnetic sheath around our bodies.

The power of our chakras is profoundly important, as their energy affects the physical, emotional, mental, and spiritual processes of human life. If a chakra is out of balance, the resulting "damaged circuit" will have a deep impact on our health, wellbeing, and relationships—in fact, the whole of our lives.

During prenatal growth, energy develops from the head down to the genital area. It is a movement from the absolute, through ever-slowing vibrational rates until we are born. Conversely, the chakras begin at the base of the spine and ascend to the crown of the head. This flow connects us with the basic instinct of sexuality and tribal significance, then ascends to the highest force of enlightenment, the supreme consciousness of the human experience. Both directions of growth are highly significant, upward forming the electrical and downward being the magnetic. As we move upward we dissolve the individual self into the cosmic self, and as we move downward we move from an awareness of "other than self" into self-awareness. Therefore, the development of the chakras has always been a major aspect of spiritual training.

Each chakra is associated with the glands of the endocrine system, an organic structure that regulates and facilitates the various functions of the body. The endocrine system is connected with the neural activity of our brain through the conduit of our spine; the openness and elasticity of the spine is essential, as the energy of our total being flows through its corridor. Similarly, the chakras act as conductors or conduits through which travels the electricity of each functioning aspect of our being. Many physical imbalances occur as the result of energy not flowing freely within one or more of the chakras.

The Seven Centers

The chakras are not easily seen, as they vibrate at very high frequencies, constantly altering with our changes of energy throughout each moment of life. However, they can be felt by those who are sensitive and seen by those who are clairvoyant, and we all have the potential to perceive them. Below is an outline of the seven chakras and the areas of our health and wellbeing that each is connected to.

THE ROOT CHAKRA

The root chakra is connected with our gonads and is linked to our basic survival needs and primitive energies—how we connect with the archetypal forces of being, such as tribal consciousness. This chakra lies deep within and without the lowest part of the pelvic area and is the source of all our energy. Stress in relation to survival creates all sorts of fearful feelings, whether this is to do with our material possessions or expression of our sexuality and the way we develop the identification of self.

Stress in this chakra may lead to elimination problems. For example, when we are involved in a threatening scenario we may be so fearful that our bowels become loose, or when we hold back from expression, constipation may occur. Often the lure of wealth, fame, or materialism arises in this chakra, leading us to the excesses of overspending. In order to curb such selfobsession or indulgence we need to learn how to recognize the meaninglessness of excessive materialism, as although this may create an illusion of security, when we trust and develop a selfless nature the reality of *true* security opens to us; SECURE: SE = SELF CURE = CURE.

Within this chakra is the Kundalini energy of the coiled serpent, the energy that moves upward through all the chakras, taking us from the mundane aspects of life to the Divine. From the basic survival conditions of fear and anxiety, we move forward creatively and grow into the experience of fearlessness and selfempowerment.

THE SACRAL CHAKRA

This is connected with the reproductive or urinary system and lies at the base of the spine. The word "sacrum" or "sacral" arises from the same Latin root as the word "sacred." From basic survival needs and primitive instincts we move to desire-based energies that link us with our primary and secondary relationships. That is, from our connection with our mothers and fathers, into significant relationships with siblings, partners, and friends. The duality of the pain and pleasure principles are at the core of this energy center. Therefore, this chakra is linked with our unconscious, the locus of man's collective and ancestral memory, and that which motivates or influences our lower nature.

Desire arises leading us to sexual or sensual/sensory pleasures. As we discover, life's pleasures never occur without pain, so stress develops as we attempt to discover a balance between these powerful forces. Pain can bring about a resistance to change, or we may choose a continual search for pleasure in order to avoid pain. These conflicting issues manifest as physical problems occurring in our sexuality or the physical locus of our sexuality. As we maintain an understanding of our sexual force in the world, we develop an ability to give birth to new levels of understanding about ourselves and the way we relate to life.

THE NAVEL CHAKRA

This chakra is connected with our solar plexus and adrenal glands and is often known as the fire center (the Hara), the focus from which our "will-power" arises. It is a center of force that leads us toward the gain or loss of will and how we master it with our ego, particularly in relation to our emotional body and its expressive energy. Therefore, from this locus arises the energy concerned with whether or not we are liked in the world. The flow or holding of these considerations leads us into an understanding of the excitement of life as well as the fear of life; the adrenals are always connected with the "fight/flight" instinct. To develop successfully in this area without becoming enslaved by one's own ego means evolving an appreciation and respect for other people. Physical problems in this chakra can often emerge as stomach upsets, when the ego of the individual loses the will to move forward in life, impeded by family restraint or professional impasse.

THE HEART CHAKRA

This chakra is connected with our thymus gland, respiratory process, and heart. It is from this center that we can feel the self-knowing of love and compassion flowing forth. Unconditional love transforms all negative emotion into empathy and selflessness. Within this chakra we may experience the true alchemy of love, when base feelings are transmuted into pure love. It is the point at which we move from basic animal survival into the compassionate understanding of ourselves and the people in our lives. The "heart attack" occurs when energies are not flowing easily through the organ of love. This is often as a result of the masculine "doing" force within our nature becoming imbalanced with the feminine "being" force. Take the middle-aged man who is a manager of stern repute but experiences the pain of heart problems through stress and overwork. His preoccupation with the doing mode has led to him becoming a "control freak" or "perfectionist," believing that nobody can do the job as well as he does it. The alternative of delegating and nurturing the talents of carefully chosen others has been ignored. However, if he were to "yield" and "let go" through trust, he would open himself to egalitarian principles that would recalibrate the flow of the feminine force he is resisting, producing a release from his heart problems.

THE THROAT CHAKRA

This is connected with all vocal expression and communication, and in the glandular system it registers with the thyroid. This locus is the primary point of interest in my sound healing work, as many of our vocal holding points arise from the positive or negative development of the energy in this chakra. Take the physical process of voice loss. This could be to do with the fact that we have expressed too much firelike energy, such as aggressive, argumentative shouting or cheering at a football match. Or it could be to do with the fact that something calls for vocal expression, and yet we are fearful of how the information may be received by those who we need to hear our frustration or anger… and so we hold back the force.

The throat is where we swallow our reality. It is a conduit between head and body and where we experience the emotions caught in our bodies; the lump-in-the-throat syndrome is a common experience, until we learn to express the energy held back. Sore throats are related to holding irritation in this chakra, when we find it difficult to swallow the realities of life.

FOREHEAD CHAKRA

This center is connected with the "third eye" or "eye of wisdom." Most specifically, it is directly linked with the pituitary gland and is the all-seeing eye that looks inward to transcendent wisdom and truth. However, some traditions believe that this chakra represents spiritual energy stepping down into the physical realm. The energy is associated with the "seer's presence of spiritual illumination," or the psychic world of other dimensions. Here lies knowledge and truthful understanding, like the objectivity and detachment of the "Renaissance mind."

From this chakra we become aware of the law of cause and effect; we awaken to the fact that all things vibrate in connection, and we learn how the spiritual laws of nature can be utilized in life, both personally and collectively.

If a stroke occurs, the energies of this chakra are severely imbalanced. Often strokes occur in the latter part of our lives—for example, when an older person is moved into a residential home. The fear and loss of independence this causes brings about change within the subtle and palpable aspects of the energy flow. If the individual can let go of the stress and fear and rebalance the energies, recovery and healing are always possible.

CROWN CHAKRA

This center is at the top of the head and is considered to be the gateway to pure intelligence or the seat of the soul; the associated gland is the pineal. This locus represents the zenith and highest purpose within human existence, connecting one-ness with the Divine. All enlightened prophets have been imaged with this chakra open and shining forth with radiant light, in the form of the halo.

Beings that ascend into the level of consciousness awakened by this chakra are exponents of the belief that there is no duality, that there is no separation between divine and mundane. This supreme experience has been called many things throughout the history of human consciousness, such as nirvana, enlightenment, samadhi, cosmic consciousness, God consciousness, or communion with the infinite. It is attained by the true spiritual master, who has washed clean or healed the contaminations within the other six chakras.

Sensing Auras: Seeing and Feeling

Everything that is animate or alive or generating force on our planet has an aura or field of electromagnetic energy. The aura vibrates within and without our bodies and is the energy field generated by the chakras. These fields of force are experienced as layers of color around each person and can be seen by the sensitive who have practiced the belief that it is possible to see them. The seven aura colors are the seven rainbow colors—red, orange, yellow, green, blue, indigo, violet—and emanate from the seven chakras. They are often emitted as combinations of color or light.

Try rubbing both your hands together with pressure; they will warm or heat up through friction. This is the electromagnetic energy surging. Now hold your hands about a foot apart and gently move your palms together and then apart, so that they do not touch but so that you can feel the force, a form of pressured energy between your hands—this is your aura.

Now rub your hands together again, but this time, as you part them, hold one hand upright, and with the other a foot away, wave the fingers of the hand up and down, facing the palm of the upright hand. You will feel a sensation rather like a cool breeze moving along the palm of the upright hand—this is your aura.

When our will and intention is strong we envelop the whole of the space around us, wrapping others in that space within the force of our aura. This occurs when the emotional field of one person is expanding through the space, such as when a famous speaker addresses a large audience. This also occurs when people feel comfortable with each other; as a result their fields of energy easily meet, or even merge into one. Of course, the converse is also true. Think back to the last time you met someone you felt uneasy with, perhaps socially at a party or in a professional situation. Did you "expand" in their company to a point of feeling easy and comfortable, or did you "contract" and feel anxious and uncomfortable?

In either situation, you were feeling the aura, or energy emanation, of that person. This is why we enjoy being with people who expand us, who allow us to feel radiant, rather than those who drain us so that we feel contracted. When we feel free we always expand and feel mobilized. When we feel fear we always contract and feel paralyzed. Sensing aura is one of the ways you can know things about people just by standing next to them. You may not see it, but you can certainly feel it.

There are seven layers or levels of energy within the human aura, and gifted psychic healers can see many of these levels. However, though most people cannot, it is quite possible to develop the ability to see the first two levels—that is, the energy of the physical body and of the astral or emotional body. By seeing or feeling someone's aura, you will be able to truly understand "where they are coming from." Obviously, this is more important for those people who are a puzzle, or for those you do not feel any connection with in a situation that demands that you do connect.

If you are feeling oddly confused or imbalanced about someone, and need to create a connection or rapport, try to sense their aura and, using the descriptions of the chakras, try to decide in which center their energy is predominant. Simply believe you can do it, and an inner picture or sensing will occur in your body/mind energy. Try to use your intuition—we all have it.

In those situations where you feel harmony with someone else, your auras are already in connection, so there is no particular need to define what is going on between you; simply bask in the joy of the connection. However, for those people we feel are complex or difficult, this "objective sensing" will help you remove yourself from the discomfort, and in time you will experience emotional intelligence, a sense of detachment rather than disconnection. In turn this will allow you to feel you are managing the situation. You will feel like a victor, rather than the "emotionally crippled" victim of the situation.

Here is a simple exercise you can try with a friend or partner in order to see each other's aura.

1. Place your partner about two feet away from a bare white wall.
2. If you are in a space with a great deal of electrical output, try to switch off all machines. If this is impossible and you can't move to another space, simply switch off all artificial lighting.
3. Stand about ten feet away from your partner.
4. Ask your partner to relax through deep breathing and to stand firmly centered, with hands unclasped at the sides of the body.
5. Now look past your partner's upper body, focusing beyond their being, at the wall behind them.
6. Concentrate steadfastly but lightly on the wall behind your partner. Try not to over concentrate and do not look straight at your partner, but rather into the middle distance.
7. Ask your partner to rock gently from side to side. As you look past their body outline you will see a fuzzy light around them. Auras are rarely uniform, so it may vary around their outline, molding into larger or smaller balloons of force.
8. Look into the light or color that you see around your partner. The more you trust and yield to the possibility, the more you will see. Can you perceive pulsations of light or color?
9. The more time you take to relax into this experience the more you will see. Don't worry if you can't see color at first; just concentrate on the white fuzzy field and color will appear.
10. Ask your partner to breathe in deeply, then slowly breathe out. You will see their energy expand as they relax into exhaling. Now ask your partner to think joyous thoughts. You will see their energy expand to as much as three feet away from their body. This is their astral field expanding, which relates to the emotional body, both in terms of pain and pleasure. At this point hopefully your partner is feeling pleasure.
11. Ask your partner to make the sound AW into the base of their spine and notice the energy grow and pulsate with the sound. Then ask them to make the sound HUM through their spine, from top to bottom. Notice the varying changes in energy and color.
12. If you do see different colors, remember their qualities—their hue and intensity—and around which part of the body they arise. These light forms will indicate much about the physical, emotional, mental, and spiritual state of your partner.

13. Link the information you have with the descriptions about the chakras (see pages 75–79) and the colors (see below). It is very important that you do this so that you can fully understand what is happening—and you *can* do this!

You can try this exercise with anyone. We each have our own individual energy field, so varying your subject will help you toward greater understanding and insight.

The colors you may see each have their own significance. The seven rays of the aura are the colors of the rainbow and are known as the primary colors. The descriptions given for each are general and not specific attunements. Our body's energies are constantly fluctuating, and therefore the "lights" or colors of our aura are also constantly changing. However, there are certain color states that may indicate malfunctions within our bodies.

RED

This color, arising from the first, or root, chakra, signifies vitality, ambition, and sexual force. If a person has much red in their aura it can mean that they are very sensual. However, if the red is dull or dark this can indicate rage, violence, self-pity, or ruthlessness.

ORANGE

This color arises from the second, or sacral, chakra and is closely connected with the way we are in relationships. If the color is bright the person is usually vitally generous, strong-willed, joyous, and warm. If the color is "cool" this can indicate conceit or pride.

YELLOW

This color arises from the third, or navel, chakra and, when bright, signifies the ability to mentally detach and analyze. A person with a lot of yellow in their aura is precise in thought, word, and deed. However, if the color is dark it is associated with states of fear, anger, cowardice, or judgment.

GREEN

This color arises from the fourth, or heart, chakra and signifies love and compassion. A person with a sense of balance and harmony gentleness and kindness vibrates through this frequency. When the color is dark it can indicate depression, emotional disturbance, jealousy, envy, or greed.

BLUE

This color arises from the fifth or throat chakra, which is associated with expression, communication, and intuition. Bright blue indicates someone who is at peace and is nurturing. Dark blue suggests the opposite: someone who may be suspicious, controlling, and possessive.

INDIGO

This color arises from the sixth, or forehead, chakra and focuses on a sense of higher values or feelings. Spiritually centered people who have strong discipline and ideals often show a lot of this color. It is associated with a feeling of self-mastery in one who is imaginative, honest, and wise and who, therefore, resonates a devotional nature. If the color is dark, perverse mental tendencies can occur, indicating someone who may be psychologically dysfunctional or contemptuous and arrogant.

VIOLET

This color arises from the seventh, or crown, chakra and, when bright, indicates a person of mystical stature. This color is often associated with great spiritual teachers or those who are connected to a pure religious practice. The energy from this chakra is the substance of relaxation and meditation and the source of inspirational energy. When the color is dark the converse is true, producing obsessiveness, unjustness, and intolerance.

There are also seven secondary colors that are complementary to the primary vibrations, and you may see one or more of these in the aura.

PINK

When you see pink—a mixture of white and red light—there is much loving energy emerging from this person. People who have dark pink in their aura can be overly modest or shy.

TURQUOISE

This color—a mixture of green and blue light—radiates from someone who is extremely dynamic and full of will. When dark it can often be associated with extreme control.

BROWN

This color—a mixture of red and yellow light—often surrounds someone who is going through a transition or life change. It can also identify someone who is stuck because of unloving negativity.

GRAY

This color—a mixture of black and white light—arises from someone who is totally "lost in a fog," depressed and unhappy, largely as a result of disempowerment.

BLACK

Black is the absence of all color and indicates the sinister, heavy features of someone who is tormented. It is associated with extreme negative force.

GOLD

This is associated with greatly illumined spiritual leaders or teachers. It is an insulating frequency, implying total integration and service, and is very special.

SILVER

Silver light exists in very high electrical force. I have seen this color above groups of people in workshops. It appears like "silver rain" and identifies high levels of soul energy, often a transcendental quality. Silver unifies knowledge with awareness.

As you become more familiar with seeing auras you will probably see mixtures and combinations of these colors, indicating the full body/mind condition of the person.

A colleague of mine referred to me a friend named Paul who was experiencing a troubled period in his life. Nothing seemed to be functioning well to create the balance that Paul wanted. He lived alone but desperately wanted a partner, and he felt stuck and unhappy in his job as an investment broker.

When Paul visited me his aura was very dull, with little radiance around his lower body. What I could see was that he lived mostly in his head or upper body, as there was much yellow emanating from his shoulder area, identifying an overuse of intellect, not uncommon for someone working in his field. Paul said he felt very gray (the color of indecision) and around his heart was gathered much deep purple, signifying to me that he was depressed. Other "lights" emanated from his being, but all were very clouded and, therefore, unclear.

We talked for some time about the constructs he could use to shift negative into positive, particularly tuning into his identification with the fact that he felt depressed. We journeyed into the nature of his depression and looked at how, by expressing his anger at the "low-ness" of his present situation, he could transform his life. I then took Paul through a deep relaxation process, finding his signature note and allowing him to visualize what he wanted to create in his life, rather than constantly fixate on what appeared negative.

A week or so later Paul telephoned me to say that he had "magi-cally" met his ex-girlfriend and that they had begun to renegotiate the troubles that had led them to separate a year before and ultimately led to his depression.

On the next occasion when he came to see me, Paul entered glowing with radiance. The heavily overbalanced yellow had disap-peared from his upper body and his heart chakra pulsated green, with magenta and bright purple exuding from his throat chakra. He told me immediately that he and his girlfriend had got back together and that he felt transformed, so much so that all his "darkness" had virtu-ally disappeared. Not only that, but he had found a way to improve his situation at work by shifting departments to avoid the immediate supervisor who had made him feel very negative.

A short time ago I had the joy and honor of meeting a remarkable man, a sacred guru and teacher of spirit from the East. This exquisite being travels the world teaching the yoga of love and forgiveness and is supported by a trust that has been founded to disseminate his teachings.

On meeting this remarkable being I was wrapped in his envelop-ing aura, an energy field of extremely broad proportions. White light spread like vapor around his being, out of which emerged bright, bright pink and green and yellow with traces of amethyst and magenta—all colors of higher states of consciousness. These colors or rays were constantly shifting, oscillating within pulsating rhythms that reached a point of stillness or pause before once more moving in other directions. I felt completely held in these benign forces, experiencing tremendous love and grace and joy deep within me, intensifying to particular richness as the swami meditated with me. On closing my eyes for a moment to concentrate on the feel-ings of love and grace, I felt my own aura lifted and cleansed by his omniscient power. On opening my eyes, the light around the swami seemed to make him disappear, when all the time his physical form was present in front of me. These were the chakra emanations of a highly illumined being.

In Conclusion...

Knowing and recognizing the functions of the chakras and the aura empowers you with great insight and understanding. Mood changes, ill health, emotional states, and feeling "stuck" or "blocked" can all be understood in the light of the body's energy centers and electromagnetic field. Using the knowledge that you have gained you will find that you are often able to recognize a person's aura, or which of their chakras is out of balance.

In the next chapter I will introduce you to sound healing—the ability to rebalance the chakras and aura using the power of sound through your voice.

CHAPTER 6

SOUND HEALING

*Sound is at the core of Creation
and as such has a hidden power,
a stupendous force, even bigger than the
power generated by the Falls of Niagara.*
—*ALBERT EINSTEIN*

Now that you have discovered your own personal signature note and developed your understanding of the chakra energy centers in the auric field, it is time to investigate the potent healing power of your voice. With the resonance of specific sounds, backed by the effectiveness of clear intention, you can use your voice to heal disharmonies in your physical presence, your electromagnetic energy and, consequently, the whole of your being. This will lead to a true energetic balance in mind, body, and spirit, coupled with a profound sense of creativity and freedom. Illness, unhappiness, disempowerment, and "energy holdings" in the form of muscular tension can be shifted and replaced by a sense of well-being, personal power, and joy.

The world of science identifies our most salient source of power as light, the light from which all life springs. This potent vibration exists through the light of the sun, the light of spirit, and the light of thought. Light brings forth our ability to consciously identify the matter of life, and sound gives consciousness evidence of its existence. All things derived from and formed by vibration have light and sound within them, so it follows that light and sound are also the instruments of our healing.

In this chapter I will take you through the steps that are useful for self-healing, starting with the identification of the problem and then using light, colors, and sounds connected specifically to the chakras to help. I will also introduce you to the delights of overtoning, a subtle and wonderful sound-making process that opens enormous healing power.

The Chakra Healing Sounds

Whether or not we can see or feel the chakras, we all have the facility to heal or purify the energy of each one. As sound is at the core of creation and as all energy vibrates, we can tune into specific sounds in order to rebalance the organic structure of our bodies.

If the body has become imbalanced through illness, emotional trauma, or some kind of upheaval in your life, then rebalancing through sound is a gentle and benign means of healing. As a result of visions he experienced during deep meditation, Edgar Cayce, the great mystic healer known as the Sleeping Prophet, said that sound would be the medicine of the future.

When our four body energies are at their purest, the vibrating light, colors, and sounds that emanate from us are also at their most pure. The opposite is also true: the duller the light, the darker the color, the denser the sound, the more bound the energy becomes within the chakras, which indicates trauma or dis-ease.

Below are the chakras and their colors, alongside the vowel sounds I have found most useful for the balancing of each chakra:

Root chakra	–	Red	–	*AW*
Sacral chakra	–	Orange	–	*OO*
Navel chakra	–	Yellow	–	*OH*
Heart chakra	–	Green	–	*AH*
Throat chakra	–	Blue	–	*I*
Forehead chakra	–	Indigo	–	*AY*
Crown chakra	–	Violet	–	*EE*

Visualizing the color, sounding with your voice, and intending a positive thought (through word, affirmation, or mantra) will help to move each center into a concentration of energy that will create far-reaching changes.

In my healing practice I often scan a person's body using these vowel sounds, made with my voice, in order to pick up where the chakras are most imbalanced and health impaired. Where there is an illness or imbalance I feel a "dullness" in the tone or vibration of the sound as it plays over the individual's body. When the chakra is alert and free, and the body area healthy, the sound automatically changes to a "brighter" and more enlivened quality of tone.

Jane's story is a lovely example of sound healing through the chakras and of the opening of the heart (love) and throat (expression) chakras. Jane was a successful businesswoman of forty years of age, who came to see me soon after the death of her mother. The nature of their relationship had been deep and multilayered. The death of someone so close is always traumatic, no matter how much we are prepared for it, and although Jane's mother had been ill for a year before her death, Jane was deeply affected.

She had "held herself together" during the mourning process by involving herself in the practical details of the funeral and other arrangements. But two weeks after the settlement of the estate and the cremation, Jane felt low in energy and "held" around her chest. She told me she had felt unable to weep and strangely disconnected from the experience.

I noticed that when she arrived Jane appeared very controlled and angry about what she was feeling. When I began to sound with my voice using the healing vowels through her chakras, I found a "dullness" in sonic resonance around her throat and heart chakras. As I created ever-increasing pulsations of sound using AH and I vowels for these two centers, Jane began to weep, at first silently, and then with a torrent of feeling.

I kept sounding, protecting her in a warmth of love from my own heart and helping her journey through the emotional outpouring until the sonic energy felt clearer and lighter. Almost immediately Jane's weeping ceased. She told me that she felt relieved and much lighter, and she was able to talk fully about what she had experienced. I was able to show her how she could use these healing sounds to bring about change, grounding her body and mind and freeing her expressive energy.

I have been able to use a similar approach with many people suffering not only from emotional blocks but from a wide range of physical conditions. I believe all dis-ease occurs holistically; we cannot separate one part of the body from another, as everything functions through interconnectedness. This is the fundamental premise of complementary medicine.

Conditions that I have helped to heal through the manifestation of sound include allergies, asthma, tumors, breast cancer, Bell's Palsy, Candida, constipation, cramp, diabetes, depression, dizziness, herpes, hyperactivity, hypoglycemia, impotence, liver problems, ME, premenstrual tension, psoriasis, sterility, and tinnitus. Through each successive treatment, the client experienced a profound lessening of the symptom, creating an energy clearing in which fuller healing could take place.

Jack was a single man in his early thirties, working as an artist for a major designer in New York. Although Jack's artwork was excellent, he had recently been ousted from a major project by a newly appointed manager in his department. When he came to see me Jack described himself as feeling powerless and angry.

He told me he was experiencing severe stomach cramps. He had consulted his doctor and had been diagnosed with colic. He had been given drugs to alleviate the pain but was still experiencing the symptoms after three months. Jack confessed that his health regime had been far from perfect. Working through the "fast track" pressure of deadlines, often late into the night, he had survived mostly by eating "junk food" and consuming vast quantities of coffee. He was fully aware that it was time for a significant change in his lifestyle and habits. He had begun regular sessions of yoga with a friend and had consulted a nutritionist.

The central locus of the cramp appeared to be around his navel area. I introduced Jack to the chakras and explained how this particular energy center is related to our personal profile in the world—our view of how we are liked or disliked by others, as well as how we ourselves like and dislike.

Interestingly, although Jack had a reasonably happy and accomplished social life, surrounded by a network of good friends, he felt a tremendous sense of low self-esteem and he hadn't had an intimate relationship for a few years. It was clear that Jack felt fear about the future, both personally and professionally, and that his health crisis had been triggered by being moved from the project he had been working on. He felt pushed aside and undervalued and was worried that his job was no longer secure.

Jack found the chakra information fascinating, and I sensed much dense yellow around his lower abdomen area, the region where he experienced the cramps. Jack and I talked about his fears and the processes he could use to adopt the opposite feeling state—joy. I introduced him to the breathing and relaxation exercises, after which I began sounding the solar plexus vowel OH. I continued doing this for ten minutes, and was aware of the dense yellow diminishing from around his abdomen and the appearance of green within this area, bringing healing.

As we worked, Jack remembered many past fears, and as he felt each one release he felt the tight cramping around his abdomen also beginning to ease. Stored emotional memories, when he had literally sucked his breath into the abdominal area so as not to feel the fear, were gradually released. After three further sessions Jack told me that he was feeling stronger and more confident than he had in many years. Soon afterward, he rang me to say he had been given a new and very exciting project to work on and that he had also begun dating a lovely woman he had met through friends.

Self-healing with Sound

Self-healing using sound is straightforward and easily achieved. You too can bathe in your own sound using your voice. As in the Sound and Body Centering Sequence (or SSS exercise), imagine you are lying down and being immersed in your own sound. Similarly, by doing this while standing upright, you can feel yourself enjoying a "Sonic Shower," cleansing and healing the whole of your body. All this requires is breath, the ability to open your mouth and sound, focused attention, the ability to physically align the spine, and trust in the knowledge that only you truly know the cellular blueprint of your being.

If you feel an imbalance in your body, such as a headache, backache, sore throat, or an emotion that you need to express, you need not endure it. Healing, gently and without pain, can be yours by your own sounding, or, because we often feel consumed by discomfort when unwell, somebody whom you trust sound healing for you.

HAVE CLEAR INTENTION

Bringing sound and color together for the purpose of healing and centering unifies the essential principles of universal force. So it is very important, before you begin the healing process, to be absolutely clear in your intention.

Remember that "thought creates reality," so think carefully about the thought or intention you wish to manifest while you are sounding. If you are preoccupied with pain, all you will create is more pain. But if you can move beyond the pain to its opposite energy (by transmuting the energy of one negative state of being into a more positive state), well-being will be manifested. So choose a positive state that feels linked to your condition and that you can use as a focus for your intention throughout the healing process.

When you are self-healing remember to use:

THOUGHT – WORD –DEED
or
INTENTION – SOUND FREQUENCY – HEALING

These three functions create a matrix of tremendous power. They alter the vibrations in the entire molecular energy of the body/mind complex, creating a potential for harmonizing every organ, bone, and tissue, and tuning your physical vessel to a frequency at which it most freely vibrates—your body's own note. As you elicit your own voiced sound, you will be transported into a "present-moment" state when mind-chatter is soothed into stillness, directing the "sound-intention" into a laser beam of clarity.

PREPARING YOUR SPACE

As we have seen, all the healing tones are specifically connected with vowel sounds. To create a sacred space for the expression of heart-centered activity such as self-healing, prepare yourself and your space by chanting the famous Eastern sound of creation, *OM* or *AUM*, or listening to another sacred sound on CD or some other form of instrumentation. It is believed that within the sound of *OM* lies the locus between Alpha and Omega, between the beginning and the end of time. By using this divinely inspired mantra you will open an interdimensional gateway between the different layers of your inner self (physical, emotional, mental, and spiritual—the four bodies), not to mention the outer energies that permeate through the universe. Your self-healing will thus be far deeper and more powerful.

THE SELF-HEALING STEPS

Make sure you have Silence, Solitude, and Stillness, just as you did for the discovery of your signature note. Before you begin, return to your signature note and try using it to release the pressure of the pain or discomfort, making sure that your spine is as aligned as possible and that you are feeling your body's gravity or magnetic pull toward the earth.

Once you have done this and have eased some of the discomfort (if you have not, simply proceed), follow, the steps below:

1. First, define where you feel the epicenter of the discomfort is, making sure that you take as much time as you need to breathe deeply and to register where the absolute core is.

2. When you feel you have identified the epicenter, close your eyes and visualize the color that you feel represents the problem, bearing in mind this is what you wish to transform. Do you see the center of the problem and what its color is?

3. If one of the secondary colors comes to mind, go to its very center and see if there is another color at its core, one of the primary colors. For example, if the pain is in your right shoulder and at core you visualize blue/green, you know the locus will be your throat and heart chakras. Whereas if you see gray, imagine you are penetrating the very fog of the gray to its center, and what do you see there? If it is white and black, go deep into the very center of what both colors provide you with, and what do you see? This process of elimination takes us deeper and deeper into the core of our suffering.

4. Take a deep, slow breath and hum gently into the core of the discomfort to assess the resonance; you will feel a warm buzzing sensation as you think the sound into the locus. Try to use a pitch that most resonates with that area of your body. For example, a high pitch will take the sound into your upper body and a lower pitch will take the sound into your lower body, as we discovered when finding your signature note.

5. Choose one of the vowel sounds from the list on page 88 (if it was the throat or heart chakra, as suggested above, you would use the *AH* and *I* vowels) and sound with your voice into the center of the discomfort. It is important to try to sound the whole of your volition or will through the vowel.

6. Do not rush this; trust and concentrate your force. In time you will notice a subtle release taking place. Savor it and take a pause to recover, then sound again. Eventually, you will feel the pain seeping from the chakra and evaporating from your being.

7. If you are in a lot of pain, this may be difficult to do by yourself. If possible, enlist the support of someone else whom you trust and allow them to do the same thing with the vowel sounds.

8. Don't forget that "thought creates reality," so if you can identify a word or affirmation that also releases the pain this will help, too. Sound crystallizes intention.

9. Remember that this is a discovery and the awakening of "the alchemy of voice," and so use the idea that is at the core of alchemy: the ability to transmute. For example, if the word that comes to mind is sorrow, it would not be a good idea to think sorrow into

the pain (this would merely create more sorrow); rather, think of the opposite of sorrow: joy. Visualize the last time you felt joyous.

10. Follow your sensing, follow your intuition—you are mostly using your right brain hemisphere in this discovery. There is no time limit, there is only the ability to create a release from the pain, a healing through alchemy.

A few years ago in Chicago I met Stella, who was plagued by headaches that often turned into ravaging migraines. She had been experiencing this problem over a period of some six or seven months and had visited her doctor, who recommended a series of tests, all of which proved negative. A course of drugs was prescribed, but the drugs only seemed to relieve her discomfort temporarily. A friend of hers suggested she attend The Alchemy of the Voice workshop.

Stella was desperate and determined; she threw herself into the work with such zeal that I was concerned. However, after extended breathing/relaxation centering exercises she became calmer and relinquished her "control" of the situation. The pressure she felt was based on a deep fear of losing control of her life, to the point where she often felt her head would explode. A long-term relationship had finished when her partner left her, shortly before the symptoms had first emerged.

When I introduced Stella to the chakra vowel sounds she decided that *EE* (the crown chakra) was the best sound to manifest and shift the feeling of "pressure against a brick wall" into what she described as "water vapor." She began to sound, very gently at first, because the *EE* has a powerful high-pitch frequency. After ten minutes of repetitive sounding Stella stopped and suggested she felt lighter and slightly like the "vapor" she was visualizing. The feeling of pressure in her head had decreased. She continued to sound and visualize after we finished the workshop, and a month or so later she sent me an email saying that she had had no recurring headaches and had recently attended a friend's party where she had met a new man whom she was dating.

John was nursing his aged mother, who was frail after breaking her hip. His mother, Lady Elizabeth, had a very agile mind, read copiously, and loved to discuss politics and art vociferously with anyone who was willing to listen. However, the hip injury had weakened her voice, and she felt unable to sustain a lengthy breath because of the discomfort. John found a way of entertaining his mother with the stories that he read, the music that she loved (Mozart, in particular), and the occasional gentle tour around Hyde Park in London.

John attended one of my workshops, wanting to seek out an alternative means of healing, other than the drugs his mother was already taking to relieve the pain.

Lady Elizabeth was very game, and on being questioned about her pain suggested it felt dark orange and was associated with the fear of losing the freedom of her meaningful relationships. Until the fall that broke her hip, she was an agile octogenarian, who always walked or drove wherever she could.

John sounded the sacral chakra (orange) *OO* into her right hip, where the break had happened. He did this once a day for a whole month, during which time Lady Elizabeth became stronger and stronger. She described the sensation as a buzzing in her pelvis, which seemed to help to knit the bone, alongside the other therapies that she was receiving. Within three months Lady Elizabeth was walking with a stick, unaided and victoriously independent.

Overtoning

Within all sounds are harmonics, and just as the name suggests, overtoning is the ability to produce the tones or harmonics that hover "over" the initial tones or fundamentals. Remember the steps used on pages 65–66 to identify the awakening of your signature note. If you strike a note on a piano you will hear a pitch or fundamental note, but if you listen very carefully, you will also hear other notes that hover over, beneath, or around the fundamental note: these are the harmonics. Overtones give sound its specific identity and unique timbre.

All harmonics are mathematically related to one another, a science that most musicians understand well. All we need to know at this stage of our development through *The Alchemy of Voice* is that overtoning has a remarkable ability to heal at all levels of our being. The harmonic sounds have an otherworldliness about them, as though a celestial influence is producing the sound. You can investigate overtoning by making the sounds of the vowel sequence from *AH* to *EE* to *OO*, sculpting the tones with your lips and tongue one after another. Overtoning, you will hear, produces a kaleidoscope of rainbow colorlike tones, which you will feel or may even see.

Goethe, the great German writer of the eighteenth century, is reputed to have said: "I call architecture frozen music." When I look at the architecture of an astonishing building such as Westminster Abbey in London or the Taj Mahal in India, I believe its highly decorated form has a powerful vibration that one can perceive, simply by lifting one's own frequency through meditation.

It takes time and practice to become proficient, so don't be disappointed if you can't master the sound-making or discover the harmonics immediately. Simply believe, trust, and have faith as you practice and the sounds will grow.

Harmonic overtones are pure sounds from the source and reflect very high octaves of energy. My firm conviction is that when these tones are used, they "key" us into an otherworldly multidimensionality far beyond the material plane of the three dimensions in which we exist, through weight, space, and time.

Kate had been a client of mine for some time when a terrible event occurred in her life. Kate had trained at the Royal College of Music in London and had sung professionally throughout her adult life, specializing in a classical repertoire. She, a lyrical soprano, had worked with a maestro in Italy and France to perfect her technique, increase her range, and open her soul to her singing and had become a successful international singer.

Kate was married to a famous conductor and had two children. Tom was eight and Victoria was five, and they lived in London, having worked abroad for most of their professional lives.

Kate wanted to open her voice, with the possibility of using it as a tool for healing. Her range was extraordinarily exquisite, and she loved the nature of overtoning. Then a tragedy occurred. Her son Tom became seriously ill with a malignant, inoperable brain tumor. The tumor was the size of a small grapefruit, lodged in the right hemisphere of his brain and growing rapidly. The best neurosurgeons in the world were treating him, but nothing could be done to arrest the developing tumor.

Kate asked me to help, and Tom, as brave as brave could be, started visualization processes to "explode" the tumor. He daily (in Alpha state) imagined flying around the tumor and sending his arsenal into the growth to destroy its voracity. Kate, meanwhile, began to overtone three times a day to help Tom arrest, overcome, or diminish his debilitating condition. Kate and Tom continued to overtone and visualize for a month, and then a miracle occurred. Kate called me and demanded I go to the hospital where Tom was. I feared the worst, but on arrival discovered the whole family around Tom's bed, where he was sitting up and looking very cheerful. Then I noticed that the swelling on his head was smaller.

Tom told me that he had continued the visualization process with his mum's overtoning, which he was beginning to imitate beautifully, until that morning, when he couldn't fire his arsenal from his cockpit. He had called in imaginary aid in the form of fellow pilots, who also flew around Mount Tumor and fired their weaponry, but nothing would function for them, either. Then he was suddenly aware of a huge explosion, which almost shattered his vision. As his mother overtoned, she was imagining that she was sending a laser into his head and literally cutting the tumor in half.

They finished the process, and Tom opened his eyes, suggesting to his mother that he had no tumor left. Kate was extremely worried that he might be delusional and called the doctor, who immediately ordered a scan, which revealed that the tumor had diminished by two-thirds.

Both mother and son were convinced that he had received divine healing, tuned by the sounded intention of both his thought process and the overtones that Kate was using as a mantra. Sound crystallizes intention.

Tom is now a healthy teenager and will be an extraordinary teacher of spiritual matters.

In Conclusion...

With a little practice, common sense, and your innate sensitivity to what is happening in your body, you, too, will identify the chakras in your body that are in need of healing or an extra energy boost. Using these simple techniques and the hugely effective power of sound, you, too, can channel self-healing through your voice and begin to bring about transformation. You will find that as a result your outlook will be more positive, you will feel more energy, enthusiasm, and confidence, and you will feel more able to manage your life and destiny. This, in turn, will lead you to make life changes—large and small—to bring about the transformations you desire and wish to create, so that you can truly live the life you want to live.

CHAPTER 7

Sacred Words and Sounds

My friend, they will return again,
All over the Earth
They will return again.
Ancient teachings of the Earth,
Ancient songs of the Earth
They are returning again, my friend,
They are returning.
I give them to you,
And through them
You will understand, you will see.
They are returning upon the Earth.
—*CRAZY HORSE, SIOUX CHIEF, 1860*

There is a powerful mystery within the repetition of sacred words and sounds, for as the repetition occurs, the intention behind the sound intensifies, thus increasing its potency. Sound crystallizes intention.

This belief has been practiced for centuries by Hindus, Buddhists, Jews, Muslims, Catholic Mystics, and Zoroastrian Parsees, who have repeated within sacred sanctuaries chants, mantras, prayers, or single words about God's powerful nature, often thousands of times a day. This intensity of action re-creates the purity of the thought at the center of the word; as the intention sounds, a powerful possibility is brought into creation. When the resonance of the intention occurs again and again it literally relives its original purpose, and thus the word or chant becomes alive with the voice of spirit.

"In the beginning was the Word" has always been a phrase that awakens this promise; it is a Christian mantra for the power of sound. Just as light creates vision, which reveals what we perceive, sound moves that vision; it vibrates form or matter and changes its relationship with the seen and unseen energies of mind and body, so that sound allows us to see spirit.

Therefore, within the "blueprint" of sacred sound lies a primal story regarding the transformation of man. Just as our DNA provides for our biological development, so these magnificent sacred words call us to our spiritual development; they inscribe a code within our souls. They lead us to the enlightenment that our collective consciousness calls us to awaken. This encoding crosses all cultural divides and all periods of history. Remember the prayers, hymns, or religious songs and chants you uttered as a child? Even if you are no longer actively engaged in religious activity, on occasions of merriment or sadness the sacred words of your childhood return to you. I particularly refer to those occasions when we all participate in fellowship, such as baptisms or funerals, the Christian Church festivals of Easter and Christmas, or the Jewish festivals of Yom Kippur and Passover.

Sacred words originally arose from organic states of feeling concerning the nature of man/woman's relationship with God. They were created through group participation to praise and petition, assisting human beings in evoking God's presence—to bring man closer to God. Therefore, these words were full of the power of man's passionate feelings about the Creator.

In contrast, modern languages are founded on principles of grammar that often move us into intellectual frames of reference rather than taking us toward the creation of feeling in sound.

The soul language of human beings is the language of pure feeling, whereas the world of intellect and information has a language based on concept, whereby we move only from the sound to the image. Conversely ancient peoples cultivated the notion of feeling through psyche or breath as a science and understood that voiced sound through the "wind of the soul" (*pneuma*) was the quintessence of life.

Whenever sacred succor was required, ancient peoples sought out a sacred space or place. These were places of refined natural energy mostly associated with Mother Nature, for example, Avebury Henge in the United Kingdom, Mount Shasta in California, or Ayers Rock in Australia. For centuries, the circle of standing stones known as Avebury Henge has been a place of pilgrimage, where our spirits can be renourished. There are many special sites like this throughout our seen world, and later in this chapter we will create our own.

From the outer to the inner, through the repetition of vowels and consonants, ancient peoples touched within themselves those energy centers connected with intuition and finer feeling—the centers we now know as the chakras.

Today, we can still use the power of certain sounds to intensify the potency of intention—the action behind the sound. In other words, we can all use chanting or repetitive phrasing to create and support the moods, beliefs, and behaviors we choose and to balance ourselves in mind, body, and spirit. A simple example of this arising in our everyday lives would be the unconsciously repeated negative "I am so worried," which brings about or supports the reality of "worriedness." One can literally see the face and body of the speaker becoming more and more frenzied with concern as they repeat their worry, and this is only the outer surface of their being. What might this worry be doing to them internally? Contrast this with the amazing uplift of the young person in love—every breath, every syllable resonates the harmony of their joy as they proclaim to the world: "I'm so happy, so in love!"

Threefold Harmony

All ancient cultures celebrated their teachings through the harmonies of sacred sound, whether through chanting mantras, singing hymns, praying stories, or speaking the names of God. These were considered the "songs of the absolute," or the "threefold songs of the universe." They were made up of three parts: harmony, rhythm, and melody.

Great significance lies in the number three: it is believed to be the vibration behind all manifestation (we often say, "things happen in threes"). The Tarot cards, for instance, reveal that number three is the energy of the Empress, which represents the part of the unconscious mind that produces growth through imagination. (Remember that Einstein said, "Imagination is more important than knowledge.") The Empress sits pregnant, surrounded by abundance. Number three is associated with the activity that creates manifestation or brings about positive change. It is growth, freedom, expansion, self-expression, and luck. In Christianity ,the number three is represented by the great triumvirate of the Father, the Son, and the Holy Spirit; in the Far East, we may see the same configuration in Shakti, Shiva, and Vishnu, and in Judaism with Jehovah, the Elohim, and the Shekinah.

Within the triad of harmony, rhythm, and melody, each has a vital part to play. From harmony arises a concord of sounds that leads to true spiritual power, as at the center of all spiritual force lies the love that manifests balance in all living things; it is the core purity of the universe, the love light circuitry. This is the first great principle of sacred sound. From rhythm arises all motion in the universe; it is "movement in time" created by stressed and unstressed accents meeting. And from melody, we feel the "tunefulness," or interplay, between what is divine and what is mundane.

Rhythm is the very pulse of life. Since time immemorial the great poets, musicians, and storytellers have used the Iambic classical rhythm that is the very heartbeat of our lives—DE-DUM, DE-DUM, DE-DUM, DE-

DUM, DE-DUM—five pairs of unstressed beats followed by stressed beats. This is called a pentameter and suspends a line of thought through ten syllables:

> *When to the sessions of sweet silent thought*
> *I summon up remembrance of things past*
> —*WILLIAM SHAKESPEARE*

This is very similar to the rhythm of the shaman's drum, which can induce an altered state of consciousness, establishing a bridge between the seen and the unseen worlds. Rhythms are capable of stimulating our biochemistry to the point of entrainment, that is, when we hear a powerful rhythm such as drumming, our bodies move into synchronisation with it, blending our own vibration with the sound that is so externally powerful.

Melody is formed when one tone is placed alongside other tones. It is defined by this relationship between tones and cannot exist without rapport. Take a mother soothing her child by rocking and humming softly. The activity caresses and soothes the child—as a sympathetic resonance is set between mother and child, a balance or synergy is created.

The unification of these three forces creates infinite manifestation in sound. By using the most appropriate combinations of harmony, rhythm, and melody, we can stimulate a powerful resonance within our bodies that will correct any imbalance, whether physical, emotional, mental, or spiritual. We all know the experience of being out of sorts with our lives, when we feel depressed or sad or anxious, and we often refer to this state as "being out of sync with ourselves." Similarly, we know when we are "in harmony," because we say "that rings/sounds true," and what better pleasure is there than being within the melody of the sound we hear.

Sound Healing and the Mysteries of Life

Sound as a means of healing possibly began in the ancient mystery schools. These schools were created to explore and teach the fundamentals of life, which often included the mysteries or secrets that are given to us in the special times of our lives, such as the moment when a child is born. These occasions fill us with the awe of what life holds; in a fraction of time we feel the enormity of life's potential.

The first great Greek mystery school was founded by Orpheus (whose name means "he who heals with light and sound") in the sixth or seventh century BC. It is written in ancient books that Orpheus had the ability to tame wild animals and to make rocks and trees move by the sweet nectarlike music of his lyre. Orpheus also persuaded Hades (the God of the underworld), through the beauty of his singing, to free Eurydice, whom the God had captured. In praise of his exquisite power, Orpheus was commissioned by Odysseus to sail with the heroic band of sailors known as the Argonauts on their epic voyages. On one such expedition they came upon the Sirens, who mesmerized sailors by their singing and led them to their deaths. Orpheus beguiled and tamed the Sirens with his own ability to entrain with sound.

His legacy was taken up by Pythagoras, who established a school of original thought in Crotona, Italy. Pythagoras taught the development of wisdom as life's main goal—he believed that wisdom is the force that is gathered from within, while intellect is that which is acquired from without. Pythagoras taught that through the act of learning the student is awakened, and that through knowledge there is purification. Later the student gains wisdom, which transcends into perfection.

Wisdom was believed to be a dimension of consciousness through which enlightened souls could perceive the purity of the word. The word is the body of the idea and the idea is the soul of the word, constantly unfolding and enfolding within its own force.

At the core of Pythagorean teaching was the philosophy of numerology. Pythagoras believed that numbers were living, qualitative realities, and that by numbering or identifying all things quantitatively we may see God's breath or *spiritus*, whether this be in the planets and stars or within the animation of the earth. Through numerology he developed an understanding of music and harmony, which was synthesized into four principle parts:

    Arithmetic = number in itself
    Geometry = number in space
    Music = number in time
    Astronomy = number in space and time

The unity of Pythagorean number theory led to the eventual development of the diatonic scale on which Western classical music is based. Like Orpheus, Pythagoras used music to cure disease emerging from imbalanced emotional, physical, or mental states and developed an exact science through which music healed illness.

It is believed that the sounds of the diatonic scale—*Do Re Mi Fa So La Ti Do*—came from heaven.

Do	*Dominus* (God the Creator)
Re	*Regina Caeli* (Queen of Heaven or the Moon)
Mi	*Micro cosmos* (the Earth)
Fa	*Fatus* (Destiny or the Planets)
So	*Sol* (the Sun)
La	*Voie Lacte* (the Milky Way)
Ti or Si	*Siderial* (the Stars, Galaxies, or Cosmos)
Do	*God I Dominus* (God in Humanity)

Additionally, it is recorded that Pythagoras said: "The seven heavens (planets) each sounded one vowel down to earth and so became the creation of all things that be on earth." In recent times, astro-scientists have studied the orbital velocity of certain planets using advanced investigative principles and have found that certain sounds can be equated with specific planets and their movement.

Joachim Marz, a clinical music therapist at the University of Basel, Switzerland, recently invented a "Sound Healing Table," which was inspired by Pythagoras. This is his description of how it works:

"The patient lies on the table, beneath which is a large barrel-shaped resonance box lined with some fifty-odd strings. As the therapist plays the strings, the emanating sound resonates through two holes on either side of the patient's head and one at the base of the spine. People who have tried the process have reported an enormous variety of responses, mostly around the theme of tranquility and well-being. The table has been designed to generate a series of notes and harmonic overtones that resonate harmoniously with the body. The strings are tuned to the pitch of A and D. A is the higher tone, which induces ethereal and sometimes out-of-body experiences, while D grounds or earths the body, penetrating it with deeper vibrations. When these notes combine a series of harmonic overtones is produced, transferring vibrations to the mind, body and spirit and enveloping the person in healing energy."

Another major breakthrough in the field of sound healing has been introduced as bioacoustics. The word "acoustic" is derived from the Pythagorean schools and means the science of sound, or what can be heard. Bioacoustics aids healing through the belief that each person emits a non-verbal sound called the "signature sound," which reflects the psychological and physiological status of the individual. Computer technology is used to calibrate the individual's "sine waves," which are beyond human hearing. When the body is out of balance, so are the waves; by rebalancing the waves the body's balance can be restored.

Vowel Sounds: the Master Code

The five vowel sounds A, E, I, O, U (*AY, EE, I, OH, OO*.) have long been associated with mysticism and spirituality. Number five in the science of numerology is the vibration behind communication. Among ancient societies it was believed that these vowel sounds hold a master code, providing us with the potential to connect with certain supreme states of consciousness and, therefore, a way to access the Divine; they may even stimulate DNA processes as they act as cellular enchantments. Certainly, these vowel sounds are "seed elements" in the sound of many languages.

We know that many Native American shamans use the five vowels as sound energies for transformative purposes, because it is felt they accomplish a great connection with the spirit world and, therefore, a healing of mind and body.

In addition, many indigenous tribes use the master code for powerful healing purposes. They use combinations of repetitive sounds to affect particular areas of the body, rebalancing, and harmonizing the affected organs.

I have been told that Native Americans use the master code vowel sounds as follows:

A (*AY*)	Connecting with the heart/chest area	North/Earth
E (*EE*)	Connecting with the throat area	East/Air
I (*I*)	Connecting with the head	South/Fire
O (*OH*)	Connecting with the abdomen	West/Water
U (*OO*)	Connecting with the lower body	Ether/Infinity

Specifically, the Pueblo Indians of New Mexico in the American Southwest use the master-code vowel sounds to connect with certain acts or states of being, such as:

AH Washing, to cleanse the individual
AY Relativity, through the understanding of all things being connected
EE Clarity, connecting with divine intelligence
OH Creating innocence and curiosity
OO That which lifts into God's presence

Vowel shapes produce tones, which then form the harmonic patterns that we know as overtones. These tones, in turn, create the timbre of our voice, with all its color. If the vowel is sung or chanted, the tonal pattern and color can be more clearly identified. For example, try saying "Alleuia" (*ahlay-oo-ya*), and really spread each vowel into a continuous unfolding, a spread that reaches through a vowel spectrum of *Ah-Ay-Oo*. Now try the same thing, but this time on a comfortably sung note from your heart chakra or signature note, sustaining or sculpting each vowel distinctly through a long, easy breath. You will feel and hear the fundamental tones and overtones gliding together; this will happen particularly on your lips, although you will also feel the tongue gliding some of the tone.

The resonance of each tone is based on a simple principle: the smaller the orifice—your lips or throat—the lower the pitch; the smaller the resonator—the mouth—the higher the pitch. These notes arise in our mouths and fall in the throat.

The word *Alleuia* means "Glory to God" and spans the spectrum of vowel tones that we humans produce (the nearest original English spelling would be "Hallelujah," recorded as probably arising in the English language around A.D. 1200). It is an Abramic chant, reaching back to the history of the Hebrew people, and arises from the esoteric practice of Kabbala, an ancient discipline at the center of Jewish rabbinical teaching. Within Kabbala is the belief that vowel sounds give words their spirit, allowing the sounder to connect with powerful, magical forces.

Enchanting through overtoning was first believed to have been created by Mongolian and Siberian shamans and is used extensively within Tibetan Buddhism. These rarified sounds help to cancel needless mind-chatter, holding the user or listener in moments of pure thought stillness, which in turn affect our mind, body, and spiritual energy.

Tibetan belief considers the voice to be a passageway or conduit between mind and body, with the voice as mediator between the physical realm of the body and the spiritual realm of the head—a bridge between the material and immaterial. Since the fifteenth century, a form of throat chanting has been practiced by Tibetan monks as they worship. This has a powerful effect on mind and body again allowing the individual to experience full sentient presentness and voiding the mind of "chatter."

Similarly, in the Islamic *muezzin,* or call to prayer, harmonic toning is used to mediate the secular with the sacred. In this case, the muezzin, taken from the Moslem holy book of the Qur'an, is intoned from the minaret of the mosque. The male singer produces high-pitched notes by directing sound through certain hand positions on the head, often through a falsetto tone. It is believed that this transports the prayer to distant locations, where it is heard as a "sweet pure stream," connecting the singer with a divine state.

In the Christian Church, Gregorian plainsong chanting was developed during a period of approximately 800 years, from A.D. 600 to 1400. This form of song arose from the direct papal authority of Pope Gregory I, hence its name. Always sung in liturgical Latin, its particular nature was established by monks singing in unison; through the elongation of vowel tones, subtle overtones are produced, changing the rhythm of mind and body.

Mystical Power Words

Ancient teachings celebrate the wisdom that certain words act like magnets, whether these words are blessings, invocations, statements of praise to instil courage and power, or sonorous charges to relieve sickness. Out of respect for this, the ancient Greek Pythagorean school students were not allowed to speak for the first five years of their education or training. Silence was considered to be an inner space of preparation before wisdom could be sounded, while listening made one observant and humble to nature. Through this experience, students were taught to dispel casual methods of speech and focus their minds away from superfluous mind-chatter toward inner content, and then to specify the reason for expression. After such an education the students were reputed to speak from their essence. The Greek mystery teachers referred to this as imparting the Logos, or Word. The Logos was the energy of cosmic reason, regarded by the ancient Greeks as the source of world order and all that is intelligible. They believed that the will of God resonated through the Logos as a self-revealed thought, and when this force entered the disciplined expression of the student, cosmic reason became crystallized within the spoken word, as though the very name of God had been uttered.

All ancient names of God and principal holy words transmit their own specific essence and are signals to evoke the divine force within the universe. These powerful word forms have within them the power to touch primal areas at the core of our beings and can, therefore, be used to open deep levels of consciousness, enabling us to make a direct connection with the God force and to tap into our own higher energy and power for transformation.

I recall once facilitating a "The Alchemy of Voice" workshop in Connecticut in the United States. During the work I told the participants that within certain orthodox religious practice the name of God would only be produced by the priest or monk or rabbi in a sacred space. A member of the workshop asked me to illustrate what this meant. I suggested that this notion needed to be fully respected by us all and that if I mentioned the name of God in the Jewish form (there were a number of Jewish people present), his presence would be evoked. The group were so pressing that I agreed to speak His name. I suggested that we be prepared for anything; we were, after all, gathered in the name of our collective spirit, examining that essence that is most pure to us—the *spiritus, pneuma,* or animating principle of the universe.

I took a great breath, feeling that in some way I was being given permission, and needed to honor my colleagues, and sounded through my note "Yahweh." At this moment, the double doors of the hall in which we worked flew open, and we all felt a chill run down our spines. At the same time, as we were near the coastline, a squall arose outside, beating wind and rain against the windowpanes. This was an awesome experience and left the entire group with a profound respect for the essence of our endeavor.

Cosmic law cites that "thought creates reality." When we chant the name of God or a powerful mantra or affirmation, we become one with the energy chanted. Through this, a cleansing or purifying takes place within our physical, emotional, mental, and spiritual bodies. When we repeat a thought out loud we connect with the collective unconscious from which the thought first arose. The more we engage in the act of repetition, the more powerful it becomes. Through this we become a minute reflection of God and the universe, in that we embody the earth and the heavens. The sound vibration connects the mind, the body, and the spirit through the conduit of the spine and the sounding of our note; in this way, we become whole.

To follow are some of the best-known mystical power words.

AMEN

This means "so be it truly." It is used extensively throughout Christian and Jewish religious practice, but originates within the Egyptian civilization. Amen-Ra was worshipped by the ancient Egyptians as the Sun God, the cosmic force that created life within the universe and on earth. The quality of the force behind the word is both masculine and feminine, the father and the mother aspects behind creation and birth. When these energies are evoked a fusion is made, bringing forth life within ourselves and the universe.

OM OR AUM

These sounds exist within the Buddhist and Hindu traditions and correspond with Amen. Very specifically, they represent the vibration of the divine word, and are believed to be the mother of all mantras. Within the sound harmonic of *Om* lies the Alpha and Omega of all creation; it is sound within sound. There are many ways of sounding the Om, each with its own specific message, or vibration. Om is the sound of our release from the physical into fuller connection with the Divine.

OM MANE PADME HUM

This translates as "the jewel in the lotus" and is used extensively throughout both Hindu and Buddhist traditions, symbolizing divine compassion. It is particularly connected with the Goddess Quan Yin (Green Tara in Tibetan Buddhism), a devotional evocation of the Divine Mother, similar to the Western icon of Mary, Mother of Jesus.

Sound Healing Temples

Sound healing temples or chambers are located around the world, some of them on ancient sites, some more recently constructed. These are sacred places where the quality of sound can be used to heal and rebalance us in body, mind, and spirit.

In his beautiful book *Being and Vibration,* Joseph Rael, a powerful shaman from Picuris Pueblo writes about sound healing chambers: "The chambers are our caretakers, helping us to access wisdom from an ancient source. They act as a mouthpiece for the higher mind to amplify that which we need at this time on earth and to help all who walk upon her. By building chambers on the surface of the earth a web of light is created so that a person making sound inside the chamber sets up a continuous resonance around the earth."

The actress Shirley MacLaine, in her book *It's All In The Playing,* writes of an experience she had when visiting the sacred Inca city of Ollanyait-ambo in Peru. She found herself being mysteriously led by an unseen force to climb a section of the ancient citadel that lay far from the usual tourist route. It was an arduous climb, and as she scaled the lofty heights she felt a powerful energy fill her entire being, willing her on to reach a tower marking the zenith of the citadel.

On reaching the zenith she found a compact courtyard containing a series of stone pillars. Within the pillars were niches, waist high from the ground, which Shirley felt compelled to lean into. Somehow knowing what to do she began to hum and then to chant the sacred sound "*Om*." The amplification from this resonated around the enclosure and through her whole being, touching both inner and outer. It transported her to a parallel level of consciousness, whereby she experienced the sublime truth of a connection with "all that is and ever shall be."

This experience confirmed for her that this site must have been an ancient temple, used for sound healing in the way described by Joseph Rael.

Jonathan Goldman also experienced the power of sound chambers; in his excellent book, *Healing Sounds,* he tells of a visit to Palenque in Mexico, where the Mayan civilization had once built a mighty city, with buildings reminiscent of ancient Egypt. In one specific temple, Jonathan was escorted by a guide into a subterranean vault, and as he was known to be a sound specialist, was asked to sing. The guide extinguished his torch, and the group was pitched into darkness.

Jonathan began to chant, whereupon the vaulted chamber became illuminated by a subtle light, enabling the outline of each person's form to be seen. Jonathan suggests that, although this was an extraordinary experience, it was not the same phenomenon as sound transmuting into light, which is scientifically proven fact, but rather specific harmonies creating fields of light. He explains that quartz crystals, such as those found in the chamber, are "acousto-luminescent"; that is, they convert sound waves into light.

At present about twenty sound healing chambers have been completed around the world.

Self-Healing through Sound

Although in many instances this form of healing is best done by someone who is experienced in the use of the voice, or who has trained in sound healing as a result of their "calling," it is entirely possible for you to practice sound healing for yourself.

In truth, we can all engage in the self-healing properties of our own voice, just by the conscious awareness that this exists, rather than simply taking our voice for granted.

All you need to do to begin is to set aside some time during your day to experience the sublime practice of "awakening" your voice. Follow the suggestions made in earlier chapters, such as the "Sonic Shower," or sounding *Om* to your favorite piece of music. By following any of these practices you will feel a wonderful sense of balance, of stillness, and a feeling of being present with life. This always brings "detachment," or objectivity, from the stresses and strains of life.

Alternatively, acquire a singing bowl from a store that sells musical instruments from the East. These bowls, when rung, give off different tones, according to the nature of each individual bowl, that create powerful reverberations. The tones of the bowl will help you to use sound as a tool with which to rebalance yourself or the atmosphere of your home. Do not worry about which bowl to use. Follow your finer feeling (intuition) and you will find the right bowl for you, as you sound it in the store.

Joining a choir may also be important to you, or listening to your favorite music. Otherwise, try to bring friends together regularly for sonic exercise, in which you help to tune each other's notes and open the chakras through their vowel sounds.

CREATING YOUR OWN SACRED SPACE

It is important that you create your own sanctuary for the sensitive process of making these refined sounds, so that you truly benefit from all the dimensions of the experience. Whether this is a room in your home, an area in your conservatory, or a power spot in your garden, find a site that feels completely conducive to the spirit of producing these sacred chants.

1.   Dress the area with sacred or inspirational pictures and colors that you feel are in tune with your energy field and, therefore, the space. You may wish to include the chakra colors.

2.   Make sure you are not near any strong electrical equipment—remove your computer or any other machine from the space—as electricity can sever the subtle higher energies created.

3.   You can create a shrine, an honored or hallowed place, by deciding what your spiritual focus is in life and displaying a picture or ornament, statue or plant that embodies this connection. Burn a candle to reflect the purity of the light force in our lives, as all life is created by light. Many people have crystals around their shrines. These help to purify the ambience as they have consciousness and can store thoughts.

4.   Have a small music center to play inspirational music, or you may prefer a musical instrument, an energy chime, a wind chime, or a singing bowl. All these devices will help you purify and enhance the space by releasing negative thought energy from within it.

5.   Decide which direction (North, South, East, West) you would best like your power space to be located in. Arrange the furniture or cushions to accommodate these directions.

6. Make sure that you will not disturb anyone or be disturbed when making sound.

7. Choose a sonic chant and enjoy sounding. By repeating one of the chants again and again you will experience a shift in force that will alter you and your sacred space into a divine vibration; what better way to rebalance or heal your energies, particularly when you have a headache after a pressured day!

Sacred Chants for Healing

The important thing to remember is that these sounds can be repeated on one note or a combination of notes; be creative and sing your own note and your own melody. These will be the song of you, the song of your soul. Alternatively, borrow tunes from famous pieces of music that you know.

OM

This is the mother of mantras and brings great peace and abundance. *Om* is the sound of sound meeting within sound. It is the still meeting point between the Alpha and the Omega, a space in which true divinity sits and where we may bring our human vibration in a meeting with that which is divine.

SAT NAM

This is a seed mantra that means "truth is thy name." Repeating this sacred sound brings healing within oneself, particularly when there has been an emotional upset and self-confidence or love of self needs to be regained.

RA MA DA SA SA SAY SO HUNG

This is one of my favorite mantras. It translates as "Sun – Moon – Earth – Infinity – All that is infinity – I am thee."

These sounds and vibrations alter the space-time continuum and bring healing from a point of stillness that exists in a dimension of "no time," where the sacred lives. You will find that this mantra improves health and strengthens resolution, as within the eight sounds exists the energy of the Kundalini. Kundalini means "the coil in the hair of beloved" and arises from the Far Eastern sacred language of Sanskrit; the Kundalini symbolizes the uncoiling of the inner awareness of our spiritual nature. This is a yoga, or "union," with the Divine.

OM NAMAH SHIVAYA

This mantra literally means "I bow to Shiva, I bow to my Inner Self." Within the repetition of the syllables lies a gradual purification of all the elements in our body. The mantra has the power to grant abundance and spiritual realization.

I AM – I AM –I AM HERE NOW HERE

This is a powerful mantra for the Age of Aquarius, the age of enlightenment that we are currently journeying through, and is one of my regular practices. Through sounding it we bring ourselves into the relativity of present time; that *now* is when we create—not then or whenever!

Anna was in deep grief. She had just experienced the most profound loss, that of the death of her two children, twin boys.
When she came to me she was in shock after hearing that her children had died in a car driven by a friend, on the way to visit their grandparents. She found it extraordinarily difficult to make any sound or to express any of the energy that was bottled within.

Grief is extremely difficult for most of us to bear, and when the loss is of one's young children through tragic circumstances, the shock of the loss is often accompanied by terrible rage at the futility of what has happened. This was certainly the case with Anna.

However, she was resolved—sound healing was her cure—and so we worked on releasing the coils of muscular tension around her heart and throat chakras. As usual we used the healing energy of the breath, warming and quietening the troubled rage in Anna's body. Tears flowed copiously, of course, and washed much of the emotional debris from her as I sounded the vowel sounds attributed to the heart and throat energy centers. Eventually, Anna was able to join in. But Anna also needed to be reconnected in herself with the source that provides all succor: the sacred. I suggested to her the two chants of *Om* and *Sat nam*, which I asked her to use three times a day, or whenever she felt she needed to be reconnected with the energy bank of the universe.

This she did, and a week later she returned with this story:
"I was humming and chanting *Om* for about twenty minutes one evening when Peter (her husband) was out at a meeting. The early evening was often the worst time of day for me, because that's when the boys died. I was sitting in the conservatory, where I like to meditate, and as I sounded '*Om*,' I felt as though a hugely warm and

THE ALCHEMY OF VOICE

very bright light was surrounding me. On each breath, with each tone, the light and warmth became brighter and brighter. For a moment I felt slightly frightened, but then just let that evaporate because I knew that the feeling was really one of awe, it was just so big I felt it enrapture me. I knew I was in the presence of something that was so loving, I ceased sounding immediately to feel it more fully. But it was as if the sound went on and on within me and outside me, even though I was not literally making the *Om*. Then, in my mind's eye, I saw my boys looking at me with such grace and love on their faces that I knew that they were in spirit, in the room with me, but full of peace and joy. This feeling lasted for a few moments but also felt like forever; in fact, I can still feel the feeling, and I know that my boys are full of joy and merging with the light. Thank you."

In Conclusion...

Sacred sounds and words, used with care and respect, have the power to heal, uplift, and enlighten us. All cultures have their own sacred sounds, and we can draw on these to find the sounds and words we feel most connected to.

Use sacred sound in your daily life to help you transcend stress, trivia, and the cerebral pressure to "do." Sacred sound can help you simply to "be." The chants will create a precious space in your life, in which to grow in knowledge, personal power, and love. The sound of exchanged thought is silver, and silence is golden!

CHAPTER 8

Words Are Organic

If words come out of the heart
They will enter the heart.
But if they come from the tongue
They will not pass beyond the ears.
—*AL SUHRAWANDI*

We use thousands of words every day to convey information to those around us, to express thoughts and feelings, and to gain a response from the listener. Most of the time, we think very little about the quality of the words we choose, or the essence of the tone we use to deliver the words. We seldom make a conscious connection between the thoughts we have and the words we express. We simply speak as the inclination takes us. Yet words are far more than simple tools of communication; words anchor states—that is, they define the emotional state we are in.

Words are combinations of sound that symbolize and communicate meaning, and in their essential form they convey the spirit of the speaker's intention. The sound of a word is a dimension of its meaning.

However, words do not always communicate what we may intend, if they are used obscurely. To camouflage someone's insecurity they can create "walls of sound" that often obliterate meaning. When this happens, all the words convey is the feeling beneath them, and the speaker will almost certainly not produce the desired response in the listener.

We have all had the experience of being "talked at" in a way that simply conveys a volume of meaningless words and feels a little like being speared or battered by shards of sound. All we can sense is the urgency, anger, fear, defensiveness, distance, arrogance, or anxiety of the speaker. Therefore, the intention behind words cannot be concealed; they will always convey the truth about a situation through their tonal quality, no matter what choice of word is used. For this reason, it is vital that we become aware of and determine our intention when we physically sound a word. When we respect, love, and honor words in this way, speaking becomes a powerful tool with which we convey immense meaning and depth. Words literally become agents of change with which we transform and shape our own lives and the lives of others.

In this chapter I will explore the origin and the meaning of words, as well as the power of the intention behind words, and what this conveys to the listener. I will look at the importance of choosing our words with diligence and care, so that we may become more aware of the way we speak and truly care about what we say to others.

The Beginnings of Language

From the very early primitive sounds made by hominids, language developed: words formed from the grunts that were emitted to convey what people felt. All words originally arose from the need to use sound to express and to convey responses about a given situation or to identify the substances of life.

In the Old Testament Book of Genesis, it says that when God had created all the beasts of the field and the fowls of the air, and because the Deity felt it was not good for Adam to be alone, Adam was charged to name everything. In doing this he gave all things "individuality," as each thing became recognized by its own name and no other word besides.

Words are a means of anchoring sensory experience and of establishing reality. When human beings agree about their value and meaning they become a shared way to communicate sensory experience. Words are crucial, they create our cultures, without which there would be no basis for society as we know it. The following extract from Lewis Carroll's *Alice Through the Looking Glass* beautifully demonstrates the power within language:

> But, GLORY *doesn't mean "a nice knock-down argument,"*
> Alice objected.
> "When I use a word it means just what I choose it to mean—neither
> more nor less," said Humpty Dumpty in a rather scornful tone.
> "The question is whether you can make words mean different things,"
> said Alice.
> "The question is which is to be master—that is all," said Humpty
> Dumpty.

The names of objects, moods, events, and creatures are not random or coincidental. Everything within the cosmos has its own note or vibration, and when we name things we perceive this vibration and find a sound with which we then shape vibrational essence into a word that we feel represents the quality of what is being named. Every name is appropriate and belongs specifically to that thing. Yes, a rose by any other name would smell as sweet, but could we really imagine calling it by another name?

Naming the things around us channels our intentions in certain directions to make sense of the environment we live in and how we think, feel, and perceive it. Ancient wisdom taught that naming created the comprehensible aspects of the thing named. The picture, the form, the density, and the feeling of a thing is held within the sound of its name. Therefore, the knowledge of everything lies first in knowing its name. Indeed, there is an ancient occult belief that to know someone's name is to share magic power over them. Plato is recorded to have said: "Names belong to things by their nature. An artisan of words is he who keeps in view the name which belongs by nature to each particular thing."

Different people have developed intricacies of naming, according to their needs. For example, Eskimo people have many different words for the one English word "snow." This arises from the many conditions that form the Eskimo's physical experience of life; quite simply, their lives depend on correctly naming the different aspects of snow, so that they can successfully distinguish the snow that is eaten from the snow that is used for building, and so on. Similarly the Hanuoo tribes of the Philippines have ninety-two different names for rice. This is their staple diet and consequently an extremely important element of their economy. English people simply know rice as rice.

Words throughout the Ages

Each generation of man has successively created new words to reflect the thoughts, wants, needs, feelings, aspirations, and desires of the experience of the age.

A powerful period of renaissance for the English language occurred around 400 years ago, in the time of William Shakespeare. Shakespeare lived in an age when words literally burst upon the world stage as never before. From A.D. 1500 to 1650, the English language flowed with new words, and during this period approximately 12,000 words were created, most of which still exist today (of course, many etymologists will debate the exact number).

Shakespeare is said to have used 17,677 words in his writings, of which one-tenth had never been used before. Of course, although predominant, Shakespeare was not the only literary force during the Elizabethan era. However, the effect of his word usage was to be long lasting. We deem his works to be "classics," which means they have a durability; this is because many archetypal features about human consciousness arise in his words, and so in his writing. As Claudius says in *Hamlet:*

My words fly up, my thoughts remain below,
Words without thoughts never to heaven go.

During the period of Shakespeare's life, only 30 percent of the population could read, and so his audience would have heard spoken words in a very different way from those which we hear and read.

Words reported to have been "coined" by the Bard were plentiful and include leapfrog, castigate, obscene, frugal, radiance, dwindle, submerged, fretful, hint, hurry, and lonely. These words are filled with sensory images and feeling states that would have created powerful and colorful "soundscapes" for the audience that watched Shakespeare's plays. Shakespeare's words reflect the age in which he lived, an age in which the sensory and experiential value of words was hugely important.

Today we also live in an age in which new words are constantly being coined. However, the words we create today reflect the technological explosion of the twenty-first century. Words such as module, info-tech highway soundbyte, personal computer, laptop, fast track, credit card, and space race have appeared in response to the needs of a society in which the value of the "spoken word" is being intellectualized and diminished by print, by pictures, by texting, and by abbreviating the formation of word feeling. We see words more than hear them.

The Influence of the English Language

The English language has become the most widely spoken language on Earth. Why should this be? Why does one language come to predominate and why does it become a common tongue between different races? The answer appears to lie in the way we hear the language.

In his book *The Conscious Ear,* Alfred Tomatis, a world authority on voice pathology, suggests that English, both today and in the days of Empire, has a particularly high frequency range, which charges the electrical energy of the brain. Sound travels in waves created by disturbed air, quantified in hertz. The range of "sound selectivity" of British English is 2,000 to 12,000 hertz, giving it a power to entrain, or the power to carry an extraordinary spectrum of meaning, which excites speaker and listener alike.

In contrast, many other languages vibrate at much lower frequencies, between 800 and 3,000 hertz, making them markedly different in their impact upon the brain and, therefore, according to Tomatis, harder to learn. This may well explain why the sound language of the British Empire was able to spread so far, and why English has become such a widely spoken language, indeed a *lingua franca* of our times.

The Sounds of the English Language

The sounds of the English language are divided into two categories: vowels and consonants. Vowels are free passages of tone, made uniquely different by lip and tongue shapes. The muscular mobility of the lips, tongue, and jaw have a strong effect on the quality and freedom of the sounds produced. These sounds, of course, change from neutral or standard placements into accents or dialects produced by the many people who share this language's heritage. Consonants are created by the lips, tongue, and roof of the mouth—both hard and soft palates—making stoppages. On release, explosive and frictional sounds are created, and in both cases the mobility of the jaw has a strong effect on the quality of the voice produced.

These different physical actions lead me to suggest that vowel tones emit feeling qualities and consonants convey intellect. What is extraordinary about these differing potentials is the action. Vowels are open flowing "organisms," while consonants are made by stoppages. Therefore, in many ways the vowels create the interior of words while the consonants provide a form to encapsulate them.

Try sounding the following sentence, in which I have substituted all the vowel sounds with the neutral vowel, or schwa, which is sounded *Uh*.

Guht suhx puhpl uhnsuhd thuh tuhxuh

You can see that all the consonants are present, providing a parameter in each word for the interior sound of the vowels. But what does it mean?

It means:

"Get six people inside the taxi"
Now try producing the vowel sounds alone:
e i EE i I uh a i

Perplexing, but try it again and see how it is relatively easier to determine meaning through the first sentence (*Guht suhx,* etc.) than the second sentence (*e i ee i i uh*). This illustrates the interior position of vowels and how they create an explosion of meaning, which is then given form by the exterior position of the consonants.

VOWELS

The five vowel sounds A E I O U are the core sounds shared by every single European culture—an astonishing fact, bearing in mind the vast variation among the European languages.

Below are the vowel sounds that are used in the received pronunciation of the English language. These sounds alter within the dialect variations in the United Kingdom and the United States. Take the English word Worcester (pronounced *Woostuh*), and compare it to the American sound definition (pronounced *WAW-ses-tuh*). The capitalized vowel sounds are long in nature, while the lower-case letters indicate short vowel lengths.

These sounds are all shaped by the lips:

OO	as in choose
oo	as in book
OH	as in blow
AW	as in law
o	as in hot
OW	as in shout
OI	as in voice

These sounds are all shaped by the tongue:

AH	as in hard
u	as in hut
ER	as in turn
a	as in had
e	as in bed
AY	as in space
i	as in ink
EE	as in breathe
I	as in sky
EAR	as in hear
AIR	as in fair
OOR	as in lure

The only tongue vowel not mentioned here is the neutral *uh* as in fath*er*.

CONSONANTS

Below are the English consonant sounds. These are shaped by the lips, tongue, and the hard and soft palate.

P/B	as in *P*eter and *B*en
T/D	as in *T*om and *D*on
K/G	as in *K*en and *G*od
CH/J	as in whi*ch* and *G*in
F/V	as in *f*ather and *v*ery
TH/TH	as in ba*th* and *th*ere
S/Z	as in *S*ue and *z*ebra
SH/GE	as in *sh*ine and vi*sion*
M/N/NG	as in *m*an, *N*an, and Ki*ng*
The Dark L	as in ba*ll* or o*l*d
The Light L	as in *l*ove or *l*augh
R	as in *r*ole
H	as in *h*ouse or *h*otel
W/Y	as in *w*ill and *y*es

The Meaning behind Words

All vowels and consonants have a physical relationship with each other, creating sound formations, like landscapes in sound, as they move into words and sentences. As all these sounds come together in the shape of speech, the meaning associated with particular sounds and sound formations becomes clearer.

Look at the two extracts below, read them aloud, and see how the sounds link with meaning. Both extracts are from Act one, Scene one of A *Midsummer Night's Dream* by William Shakespeare, and in both it is Theseus who speaks.

Now fair Hippolyta, our nuptial hour
Draws on apace. Four happy days bring in
Another moon — but O methinks how slow
This old moon wanes! She lingers my desires,

Like to a stepdame or a dowager
Long withering out a young man's revenue.

Go Philostrate,
Stir up the Athenian youth to merriments.
Awake the pert and nimble spirit of mirth.
Turn melancholy forth to funerals.

In the first extract, Theseus is wooing the captured Amazon, Hippolyta, and his language is sensual and sensory—it is the language of the heart and desire. If you try to accentuate the vowel sounds as you read what he says to her, you will discover that he uses long vowel tones that literally express the way he feels in an extremely physical way:

But O methinks how slow this old moon wanes!
She lingers my desires.

But OH mEEthinks hOW slOH this OHld mOOn wAYnes! ShEE lin-guhz ml diziuhz.

Each vowel holds within it the breathtaking quality of his desire and love. But a few moments later, when ordering Philostrate, his servant, his language changes. It becomes full of consonants, to the point of being almost percussive.

Go Philostrate, stir up the Athenian youth to merriments.
Awake the pert and nimble spirit of mirth.

As you speak Theseus's words, accentuate the consonants. They will feel short and sharp in comparison with the sounds of his earlier mood. These sharper sounds express the way he feels in relation to his servant. He appears impatient or bad-tempered and gives an "explosion" of instruction. He communicates from a different aspect of his being, more from his head than his heart.

One hundred years after the Elizabethan era and Shakespeare's prodigious work, language had organically developed into another quality of being. By this time the Age of Enlightenment had begun, and the heady function of intellect was more in fashion than the heart of the Elizabethan's emotional sensuality. Scientific advancement was the order of the day, and British society followed suit by intellectualizing even its most romantic language into wit.

Look at this extract from *The Way of the World* by William Congreve and read it out loud:

Mirabell:
> *Do you lock yourself up from me, to make my search more curious? Or is this pretty artifice contrived, to signify that here the chase must end, and my pursuit be crowned, for you can fly no further?*

Millament:
> *Vanity! No. I'll fly and be followed to the last moment, though I am upon the very verge of matrimony; I expect you should solicit me as much as if I were wavering at the gate of a monastery, with one foot over the threshold. I'll be solicited to the very last, nay, and afterwards.*

Mirabell:
> *What, after the last?*

Millament:
> *Oh, I should think I was poor and had nothing to bestow if I were reduced to an inglorious ease, and freed from the agreeable fatigues of solicitation.*

Millament and Mirabell's affection is expressed through wit and contrived through intellect. The language is structured to convey their consonantal repartee, and therefore is vastly different from the ecstatic wooing of Theseus and Hippolyta. In both examples, we can hear and so feel the spirit of the speakers' intention echoing through the sounds they use.

Exploring Sounds

What these literary examples demonstrate so clearly is that words are physical entities; they are formations that we breathe, utter, savor and "eat" each day of our lives, and, therefore, they have huge importance for us.

Yet we have become such literate beings that the printed word often takes power over the spoken word, even though the printed word has no life other than that which gives us information; the spoken word on the other hand is filled with a vital energy that can be felt as well as heard.

Try the following simple exercise to distinguish between the effect and impact of vowels and consonants:

1. Take a poem or piece of prose that you remember loving or being inspired by. Choose something that cries out to be spoken rather than simply read. Speak it out loud once. Imagine you are saying it to someone who is dear to you. Focus on them, so that you create your signature note to establish rapport and warmth and meaning. Perhaps even record this first aspect of the exploration, so that later you can see the difference.

2. When you feel you have committed yourself to the meaning of the piece and the focused communication of it, try to organize the sentences in the piece as clusters of sense. Be as precise as you can, organizing them into sections that can be spoken on one breath. This is important, as it gives shape and meaning to the sound phrase or sound landscape. Today, we often speak in very short sentences and take very short breaths, so you will probably find that your breath is taxed. Persevere and extend your breathing and speaking to the rhythms of the text—the duration of each thought.

3. To help with this, speak the piece in association with the punctuation, but try not to let your note keep dropping (a falling inflection) on the commas, only at the full stops, when the thought of the writer has fully finished.

4. If you need to find more breath and feel yourself breathing in the middle of thoughts, do not concern yourself. You could try Gregorian chanting each thought (singing or intoning on a monotone) to help find the length of the breath. This always works as you will find the "measure" of the thought.

5. Now you will have the landscape of the thoughts secure, so let's go into the interior of the sounds.

6. Isolate each word by forming only the vowel sounds. Accentuate the vowels and you will see the harmonies within the interior of the words.

7. If you can, record yourself doing this. Feel the sounds within the words giving you a sense, maybe even a color or feeling, of the meaning.

8. Now do the same thing with the consonant sounds. You will feel the parameters of the words emerging, as well as some consonants being located within the body of the word.

9. The important thing is not to rush this exploration. Allow yourself a comfortable period of time for the different sections of the exercise.

10. When you have explored each word thoroughly, try speaking the poem as you did the first time. You will notice that you "own" the words in a totally different way, feeling the life of the sounds in the words within your body. This gives them texture and weight and embodied life—as you speak the words you will feel transformed.

Giving Life to Speaking

Words cry out to be spoken, as we have all experienced. Recall an episode from your life when you found it difficult to speak, such as during a meeting or presentation or profound emotional process. In keeping silent you were able to "trap" the feeling state inside your body. Now imagine yourself speaking about the experience, even if it is painful. You will see that speaking is a release; by forming the sounds that come to your mind you release the pressure inside your body and become fully present to the condition of embarrassment or anxiety and that which heals or transforms it. When we speak we are simply dealing with energy that needs to be expressed, so let it go, for speaking is a release. That's why we say "a problem shared is a problem halved."

When we are suffering pain or sorrow we make sounds, often from deep inside ourselves. The sound releases the pain and makes us feel balanced or centered again. Don't hold sound back; it is our savior!

Julian was twenty-eight when he came to see me, after years of living in the silence of solitude. He felt alone in his own ivory tower of silence, a prisoner of his own consciousness.

Julian was intelligent and extremely well read. Indeed, the books he devoured were the only way he felt able to relate to the world. In life he was monosyllabic, speaking in grunts. But he wanted to change this and find a way of communicating the richness of his interior to the outside world; he wanted to find his voice in the world and relay all that he felt.

Julian was the only child of two academics who were brilliant in their own fields as scientist philosophers. But they were so wrapped up in the meaning of their own outpourings that as a young person he was constantly told that he did not know what he was talking about, and he was never encouraged to speak. As a result, Julian was introverted, tongue-tied, and he occasionally stammered. He produced a very depressed tone, as though he was literally "sitting on his voice."

We began the work by exercising his jaw, using very open "chewing" movements that freed the muscles that kept his jaw and mouth closed like a thick curtain. From the jaw-widening mobility exercises we proceeded to other facial isometric exercises that encouraged the super-muscles of his face to express the feeling states that had been kept unexpressed. These feelings were myriad, but step by step we found the words and balanced his facial expressions with the sound of the words, taking first the vowels, and then the consonants. All his fear, joy, embarrassment, enthusiasm, loathing, and loving came pouring out.

After two months of this, Julian began reading sections of his favorite novels to me. Seeing and hearing Julian "unlock" the stored wisdom and "be-jailed" feeling states within, and open his inspirational interior life, was like uncovering a treasure trove of profound wealth.

This enabled us to open his breath support and to focus on his signature note, which was deep and rich and melodic, and very different from the "grunts" or breathy, thin stammerings he had once produced through the fear of ridicule or disapprobation. Consequently, a handsome, kind man was born.

During our three months together Julian's confidence increased, and with it his social mobility. For the first time in his life he was magnetically drawing people to him, and he found that people were genuinely interested in his eloquence and knowledge. Soon afterward, he found a partner with whom he explored an ecstatic physical and mental connection.

Today, four years after our initial meeting, Julian is working as a voiceover artist and has truly found his vocation.

What's in a Name?

Names are particularly fascinating to study. Our name identifies us in the world, and I believe that the sound formations of our name are interpretations of our essence; we either become the name or the name becomes us. This is why we often change our name, either formally by deed poll, or informally by taking a pet name or shortening our given name.

We link our name with our identity, so that if we feel ourselves to be unaccepted by someone influential when we are young, we often respond by hiding from our true name, as if we do not wish to own it or feel entitled to it. We may hide behind a nickname or abbreviation of our essence—our very creative source.

One of the most exciting liberations I have witnessed occurred in an "Alchemy of Voice" healing workshop in North America some time ago.

One of the people attending had been struggling throughout the course of the morning's work. Her name was Shelley and she had always had a very diminished perception of self and experienced life as a challenge.

Shelley agreed that she had never truly liked her name. Her parents had always used the sound of her name in a derogatory fashion; they had been extremely draconian in their restrictions of her self-expression during childhood. Phrases like "Oh Shelley, why are you so stupid?" had been the persistent negative "mantra" that they had used, and Shelley told us that hearing these statements was rather like being pierced with knives in her solar plexus.

I positioned Shelley comfortably within the center of the circle of people who were attending the workshop. We then chanted her name benignly, holding the intentions of Love and Freedom in our minds. Sound by sound, vibration by vibration, over and over we chanted, sending much love in our force. After about ten or fifteen minutes Shelley perceptibly became enlivened, and her cloak of fragility dropped away. She moved back from the center of the circle and started singing her own name with one of the greatest smiles I have ever seen. The sound of her name reenforced, honored, recognized, and released her to her own self-knowing for the first time in many years.

Often in workshop situations, I encounter participants who have great difficulty in speaking their name to the group, as once we name ourselves we proclaim our entire being or identity within the sound; there is simply no way of hiding. Synchronizing with others in the way I have described really allows us to be nurtured into "other-centeredness," when the energy of the space is enlightened by an intention of love from the collective gathering.

Choosing Your Words

We choose very specific words for very specific occasions. There is informal speaking—the speech we use with those we are close to—and formal speaking—the speech we use in social situations that require decorum and etiquette. In some situations there is some intermingling of the two and, of course, as other social rules such as dress and manners change and evolve, so does the use of speech. As we have found earlier in this book, when sound is specifically formed, our voice crystallizes intention; sound brings life to the action of intention. We create or re-create through sound, time and time again. Therefore, it is radically important that we choose words with the greatest care and love. We all know how a few clumsily chosen words can knock someone into an emotional chasm of self-doubt and re-crimination. The converse is also true. For example, look at the joy in a young child's face when words of love or approbation are uttered.

HOW TO CHOOSE YOUR WORDS

1. Think about an important statement you need to make to a member of your family, or perhaps something within a more "formal context" at work.
2. Start by "mapping out" the key words in your mind that you wish to say. Perhaps write them down in order, to be precise.
3. Sound the vowels and consonants within the words, and decide whether they truly convey what you wish to say.
4. Do they come from your heart or your head?
5. Are you truly sounding your signature note?
6. If you feel your note behind the intention, are the words coming from one of the four body chambers we have explored?
7. If for some reason you find this taxing, do not concern yourself with perfection or wrong choosing; simply bring the sound intention through your heart chakra, which we have discovered is nearest to the position of your signature note.
8. Do you have the breath to really convey the "heart content" of what you wish to embody and enchant?
9. Try the whole statement or just the words in your head resonance. Notice what it means; record it, if you feel you need to.
10. Try the whole statement in heart resonance. Notice the difference!
11. Again, concentrate on shaping the landscape of the vowel and consonant sounds.
12. Finish by observing the tempo or rhythm of the way you say the thoughts and the sound shapes.

Use this exercise whenever you have something important to say, and you will notice how soon you will be applying these notions, without thinking, to all your words. Choose words that support, hold, and affirm others. Always avoid words that hurt, damage, or wound: negativity paralyzes; positivity mobilizes!

Problems with the Voice

In any given moment our voices reflect our physical, emotional, mental, and spiritual states of being. When there are physical voice or speech inaccuracies present, the condition indicates that the motive or objective of the individual's intention is out of balance.

Below are some of the common voice and speech problems and the possible causes. In all these cases, the problem can be resolved through the use of sound and color healing.

- When a person's diction is unclear, the condition is often related to not being precise in thought. This is an indication of a sense of disempowerment, often accompanied by a radical mistrust of words. The face of the speaker will appear bewildered, indecisive, depressed, or aggressive.
- Overemphatic speech has more to do with a lack of trust in communicating. The person literally "pushes" the sense out. Grandiloquent and "dumbed down" speech both originate from a similar root; issues to do with low self-esteem are often the cause.
- Unclear word endings with no final consonants are related to not being present with the entire thought and of not thinking through to the final moment. A fear of responsibility in the face of authority is often the root cause. Speed of thought can also be a cause, where the relay between concept and spoken word is extremely accelerated.
- A stiff jaw or immobile lips indicate a reluctance to communicate. This often occurs as a result of mistrust that the utterance will be honored and is common in someone who has been dominated by a father-figure as a child. Stammering or stuttering are extreme examples of this condition.
- Staccato speaking or "clipped" sounds (whether vowel or consonant) are to do with being afraid of feeling. Lazy or sloppy speech often arises from an individual's unconscious sense of impotence or lack of power.
- Glottal attack (cough in the throat) or breathiness is related to anxiety.
- The over-resonant voice indicates a generalized emotional process rather than specific expression of thought or feeling.

This often emerges as a "shouted" delivery, or the subtle anger of the "clenched" throat, resulting in a rasping sound. An insecure emotional life is often at the root.

- A voice that "sirens" with an overbalance of head resonance or "metallic nasality" indicates habit-formed tension. The breath is often held high in the upper chest, which can be a result of asthma or other respiratory dysfunction.

  Difficulty with breathing can result in a worried or downcast facial expression, or lack of expression. These conditions are mostly connected with the challenge of early life trauma.

- A monotonous or flat tone can often be an indication of depression or emotional repression; tone deafness can also accompany this condition, as the neural pathways become held by pressure.

In Conclusion...

This chapter has revealed that words have an enormous power, though most of the time we are completely unconscious of these powerhouses of thought and feeling. By choosing to explore and understand the words you use and the sounds you make, you can richly enhance your life and your experiences therein. Choosing the right words for a particular situation, sounding the words with care in order to fully convey the meaning, and speaking the words from your heart, through your signature note, will dramatically alter your sound and position in the world. As a result, the way you are perceived by those around you will alter. You will be listened to, taken more seriously, regarded with respect, and your opinion will be sought. Always speak the truth of your mind with passion and persona, not to afflict others or yourself but to enhance life!

CHAPTER 9

The Inspirational Speaker

The man that hath no music in himself,
Nor is not moved with concord of sweet sounds,
Is fit for treasons, stratagems and spoils;
The motions of his spirit are dull as night,
And his affections dark as Erebus:
Let no such man be trusted.
—*WILLIAM SHAKESPEARE*

Many of us are required to speak formally before an audience at some point in our lives. For some this is a regular event, while for others it happens only occasionally. Our audience may be one or two people, or several thousand. But whatever the size of audience, and whether we are called to speak often or not, most people's fears are the same.

For many years now I have worked with people in the fields of business, politics, education, religion, the arts, and entertainment. My role has been that of Master of Voice, Master of Presentation, or "Presentation Alchemist," providing active skills and support for those who are making speeches, giving presentations, pitching for business, auctioneering, leading worship, teaching, or performing. I have helped to release the fear, anxiety, and awkwardness that so often cripple the potential impact of the delivery or performance. I have encouraged each individual toward their own self-empowerment, and to discover the ability to use their voice as a powerful expression of human integrity.

In this chapter, I will examine the reasons why so many of us feel powerless and afraid when we are required to speak in front of an audience. I will explain the secrets of truly effective public speaking, and outline the steps needed to transform yourself into a confident, self-assured, and inspirational speaker. You will learn how to create a positive experience and a positive outcome, no matter how anxious you may be to begin with, and I will show you how to conquer your fears, overcome your doubts, and create a powerfully focused and unique presence.

Things That Can Go Wrong

So often people say to me, "I know what I want to say, so why can't I say it?" Despite the fact that they have prepared their material and are happy with it, speakers may become paralyzed with fright once the time arrives to deliver their efforts in public, even if that "public" is a small meeting within the company or workplace.

Below are some of the symptoms that speakers commonly report when their presentation is going wrong. See if you recognize any of them from your own experience.

1. You feel "frozen" when you see so many people looking expectantly toward you, and you feel the heightened energy in the room or arena.
2. You find it difficult to catch your breath and your voice goes up in pitch as a result of throat tension. You feel no sense of gravity.
3. Your hands become very sweaty and your knees and head shake with nerves, which encourages your tongue to stick to the roof of your mouth.
4. You feel so "high on adrenaline" that you become "nonpresent" and unfocused; in short, you do not truly see your audience.
5. You speak too rapidly and obscure your message, which often becomes inarticulate as a consequence of the tempo and rhythm of "bound" energy, rather than "flowing" energy.
6. You ignore the ambience and how hot/cold, dark/light the presentation room is, leaving the audience uncomfortable and, therefore, unlikely to pay full attention to your message.
7. You shout your message in an attempt to be heard, even if a microphone is being used, which alienates the listener.
8. You don't listen or hear clearly, and as a consequence of not being present you use repetitive "space-fillers" like "Um" or "Er." These gestures are meaningless. We use them because we unconsciously feel we need to keep doing something, rather than pausing, recovering, being still just for a moment, and then continuing.
9. You lack focus and the ability to really be authentic with your audience.
10. You block being completely open to the conversation between yourself and your audience.

These are just a few of the things that allow us to become stuck or ineffectual in presentation or performance situations. Yet all these situations can be reversed, producing instead a state of being Calm, Commanding, and Conscious. Later in the chapter, I will teach you how to exercise some of the "muscles" of superb performance, so that you will ultimately appear and feel inspirational.

The Fear of Public Speaking

Practiced speakers often appear fluent and effortless. However, this almost always means they have put in a great deal of effort first, because surveys have shown that the majority of people are more terrified of public speaking than they are of death, the termination of a major relationship, or buying and selling property. In other words, more people would prefer to be in the coffin than to give the eulogy for the dear departed one at the funeral!

These fears produce sleepless nights, physical tensions, illness, a lack of self-esteem, and a whole host of other problems and negative impulses.

Fear and doubt show in our voices because the voice is the first aspect of our being that connects the inner kingdom of self with the outer world. The voice is a quintessential part of our physical life and creative being. The terror of public speaking often results in vocal problems such as sore throats, huskiness, dryness, stammering, body shakes, a need to frequently clear the throat, a loss of vocal power, speaking too fast, being unfocused, or other more painful or serious conditions. When we are suffering from these conditions it can be very difficult to see that there is an alternative. However, if we can rethink the situation we have an opportunity to truly transform or transmute the painful condition into the opposite state, using our own personal alchemy.

Hamlet gives us inspiration with the thought: "There is nothing either good or bad, but thinking makes it so." In other words, the way you think about a situation determines the outcome. If you approach it with terror, then it is likely to be a disaster, whereas if you approach it with joy and excitement, you will already be moving yourself toward a more creative path and easier destiny. We all know that negativity paralyzes and positivity mobilizes, and it is important to remember that happiness is a decision, not a condition.

TRACING THE FEARS

My experience suggests that those of us who are challenged by presenting ourselves in formal situations often feel that we are being judged or assessed unsympathetically Time after time, I have worked with dynamic, successful people who are reduced to quivering wrecks by their fear of other people's criticism and judgment.

Several years ago I took part in a BBC series entitled *The Confidence Lab.* The series was produced after a BBC survey was carried out throughout the United Kingdom. The survey found that 93 percent of the population suffers from a lack of self-confidence or self-esteem.

The twelve members of the public we eventually worked with to create the series experienced problems such as:

* conflicts in personal relationships
* low self-esteem
* public speaking crises
* severe financial difficulties
* divorce
* emotional immaturity
* lack of promotion at work.

The production team, the panel of highly trained therapists, and the participants spent two weeks filming at a luxury country house hotel. The participants took part in motivational workshops, voice training, physical fitness exercises, and individual analysis or therapy, as well as many socially interactive processes in order to shift the problems and challenges they experienced in their lives and improve their confidence and self-esteem.

We worked with them in an atmosphere of care and mutual respect, and all who took part benefited enormously. Life-changing shifts took place, and even the production crew—known for their hard-working but cynical viewpoints—were moved by the revelations and transformations that took place. Much of my experience, both in the Confidence Lab and in my private practice, suggests that the fear of public speaking often arises from early life experience, when we have confronted a major authority figure—a teacher, parent, carer, or any other influential adult—who does not accept our behavior and who is critical, cruel, or judgmental.

By employing benign physical-psychotherapeutic skills, one can gently journey through the rich landscape of earlier life to discover whether we experienced the trauma of nonacceptance. Once the experience has been identified, it is possible to defuse the power it holds over us, simply by recognizing the effect it has had and making another choice. After all, consciousness means choice.

Frank was a highly motivated, upwardly mobile company manager. The company for whom he worked was a major player within the international hair and beauty industry, and when we met he had just been given responsibility for a new product launch. Frank's career successes were innumerable, and he was rapidly heading for a senior management position. He had recently married a very attractive colleague, was physically healthy, and had everything going for him.

But Frank was terrified by presentations, and as he was required to make them frequently, this was making his life a misery. His whole being rejected the idea that he could be a successful presenter, and when he was presenting he literally shook like a leaf.

I was called in to help him, and from the beginning of our conversation I was aware that although Frank was obviously distressed about the fact that he experienced tremors in performance, he was also very tense in the upper spinal area and shoulders, which effected tremendous throat tension, resulting in a clenched voice. I felt intuitively that he was defending himself against yielding to vulnerability, and this was confirmed by his reluctance to try "breath release" exercises, which would help him to stop shaking, release the withheld force, and open his throat. He expressed angrily that he had been given a few rudimentary breathing techniques by a personal trainer to help with the excruciating tension, but he claimed they had not worked.

When I attempted to take Frank through a relaxation process in order to release the body tension and to open his throat, he refused, suggesting it wasn't necessary.

I tried a different strategy, asking him to tell me what color he thought the "holding point" in his body was. This notion was strange to Frank, but he felt this intellectual search was easier as he only needed to connect with the imagery of thought.

He immediately replied that the feeling was dark blue/green (the color that I had already sensed around his upper spine). I then asked what sound came to mind that represented the tension in his throat during presentations (I gave examples from a written list) and he suggested a tight "I" vowel.

I asked him to sound the "I" and to imagine the dark color, which he did. He immediately began to shake and stopped sounding. I asked him if he could tell me how young he felt and if there were any memories of that age. He was very surprised by what ensued—a revelation from deep inside his cellular memory.

He told me the story of his move from junior school to grammar school at the age of eleven, and of feeling inferior during certain classes such as English and art. On one particular occasion, the English teacher chose Frank to read aloud, and when he did this the class (all boys) responded by sniggering and ridiculing him. Frank's response was to hold so tightly to the book in his hand that he shook with tension. He wanted to throw the book in the face of his opposition, but was too frightened of the repercussions. To top this, the English teacher, a man of about forty, also ridiculed him by laughing and bringing him to the front of the class. This painful memory stayed in Franks physical/emotional body, so that each time he attempted an important presentation he was unconsciously reliving the experience of his childhood.

Frank's understanding of what had happened to cause the fear provided him with a greater knowledge of how to move forward, and we began a program of sessions to develop skills not only to overcome the tremors but to open focused contact with his audience.

Frank's anger disappeared as he enjoyed both these sessions and several sessions of professional massage (having also seen an osteopath and acupuncturist at my behest), which concentrated on releasing the taut muscle in his upper spinal area. The constriction was held around the heart and throat chakras (which are green and blue in color), corresponding with the dark green/blue energy Frank had seen in his "mind's eye."

Frank realized that he had lived his whole life in fear of rejection by male authority figures, in consequence of the teacher's attitude. The work we were able to do together was hugely healing, and within three months Frank was giving successful presentations to his male colleagues and superiors with great ease. The perception of fear had been irrevocably altered.

I have come across many cases like Frank's and have discovered that while public speaking can be an enormous challenge, it is often an opportunity to heal and transform the negative into a positive.

CLEARING YOUR OWN CHALLENGES

Each one of us can clear the fears that hold us back from confident and effective public speaking. But the only way we can truly change and evolve is by first identifying what needs changing, and then taking action to resolve the challenge.

Begin by thinking of the last time you spoke in public. It might have been in front of a class, at a wedding or other social event, in a work situation or at an informal get-together. Now answer the following questions.

1. Did you feel at ease or tight and tense? Ask yourself "How did I feel?"
2. If you were tense or holding yourself tightly, where in your body were the tension points?
3. Did you feel self-conscious?
4. What do you feel went wrong during your speech?
5. What do you feel went right?
6. If you can, ask someone who witnessed your speech to give you their impression—it needs to be someone you trust will answer honestly.

The answers to these questions will give you a lot of information about what happens when you speak. Now, using this information as your basis for action, follow the self-healing guide below.

- Find a space where you will be able to create a calm and clear state.
- To counteract feelings of self-consciousness use the Silence, Solitude, and Stillness exercise from Chapter 3 (pages 54–56).
- Using the information from Chapters 5 and 6, focus color and sound healing on the points in your body where you feel most tension and rigidity during your speech (pages 82 and 88).
- Think of a word that represents the negative feelings you had at that time, and then transmute it, holding the opposite word in your mind as you use sound and color healing. For instance, if you felt fear, use joy; if you felt closed, use open; and if you felt tense, use at ease.
- Practice these exercises, and before future presentations or speeches you will be able to summon them easily to mind and tune into your relaxation process, so that within a few

minutes your mind, body, and spirit will be aligned, and you will feel yourself calm, clear, and able to give your best.

- At all times (but particularly before and during a presentation), feel the rhythm of your breath flowing freely through your entire being. When you wake to the knowledge that this day is a presentation day, start breathing deeply and slowly as you move toward the activity.
- Practice the presentation pitch, so that all your intentions can be fully supported by your breath. Human beings always have enough breath for the thoughts that we speak. This allows the rhythm or tempo of your delivery to be fully lived and moves you toward being captivating or magnetic. Avoid using falling inflections before the thought finishes. This can occur when we see a comma as a full stop, so try not to.
- Word clarity is crucial for your message to be clear, so choose the key words that you can emphasize in order to truly inform your audience. Try not to rush: this obscures your message.

Remember that your objective is not to eliminate the butterflies you may feel before public speaking, but to get the butterflies flying in formation, so that you are able to manage your nerves and can choose the action that will help you and encourage you to feel empowered.

Creating Impact-full Messages

While most people facing the challenge of public speaking are concerned with what they are going to say, the truth is that the content of the message is only one aspect of what will potentially affect the audience, and not even the most important one. Of course, it is true to say that if we do not prepare the content of our presentation we will not achieve success: If we fail to prepare, we prepare to fail! It is just that, in addition to the content, there are other aspects of the presentation that we must address in order to be truly effective.

How do we know we have been effective and achieved what we wish? All successful communication is based on the response one receives. This means that if you are successfully communicating, you will receive the desired response. The converse is also true: if you are not successfully communicating, you will not receive the desired response. This is the essence of "response-ability" (the ability to respond). If someone is "irresponsible," this means they simply lack the "ability to respond." We tend to complicate this process by assuming that irresponsible individuals are churlish or awkward; the truth is that they often do not know how to respond because we haven't made it clear to them what we expect.

Neuro-Linguistic Programming (NLP) offers a paradigm or model of what all successful presentations are based on. According to NLP research, what the audience responds to is:

- Body language: 55 percent
- Voice tone: 38 percent
- Content: 7 percent

It is quite clear, therefore: It is not what we say but how we say it that really matters. And since body language and tone of voice are clearly just as important as the content of your presentation, you will need to pay attention to them and to learn how to communicate through these channels. Using body language and tone, you convey the essence of your message and your own true authentic note.

Being Present and Supremely Focused

One of the most important aspects of overcoming the fear of presentation is to learn to be truly present. This brings focus, presence, and eventually other qualities that are described as magnetism, charisma, aura, and star quality. I believe the only way through which we can experience these extraordinary states of being is by creating our "actions" through stillness—stillness is at the core of powerful people's lives; it is the route to power.

Look at one of the most powerful natural kinetic forces that exists on earth: the hurricane— hundreds of miles of whirling energy vortex creating mass destruction as it travels. Go to the very epicenter of the hurricane or tornado, and what do we discover? In the very eye of the storm is complete stillness; it is from this stillness (feminine force) that the extreme dynamism (masculine force) emerges.

Therefore, in order to find a center in our lives, in our work, or in our presentations, we need to discover how relaxation and stillness can inform us. Practice the Sound and Body Centering Sequence (the Silence, Solitude and Stillness exercise) in Chapter 3 (pages 54–56). At the end of the sequence, notice how open your senses are. Our senses mark the very edge of our consciousness. When we are not "present," each sense moves from self-awareness and openness into a "closed-down" state for personal inner reviewing. We call this self-consciousness, and when we do this we do not focus clearly on the people whom we are relating to and our bodies become uncomfortable and uncentered. We find it difficult to breathe, we talk too fast, and we use erratic, unbalanced gestures, which in turn unbalance our audience—in short, we do not focus on the listener because we are only focused on ourselves.

Focus means the way we *attend* to the *intention*. The word is derived from Old English and means "hearth" or "light source." Can you remember the last time you were near a fire, whether in your hearth at home, at a firework display, or sitting around a campfire? You were almost certainly drawn to this source, at times transfixed by it and totally focused on it. Even the television is a form of "light source," and we all know how everyone becomes transfixed by this "light-box" until someone switches it off, and then conversation begins.

This is what happens with great speakers. They become "enlightened" with their own force and the positive audience energy that feeds them, so that the audience is drawn magnetically to them and focuses on them.

Toward the end of this chapter, I will give you a simple exercise or procedure whereby you, too, may become a force of light that illuminates people's hearts and minds and spirits. The principle begins with enjoying yourself!

Presentation Embodiment

When I train a person or a group of people for public speaking or presentation situations, I encourage an understanding of the core values that sit at the center of the word "presentation." A useful maxim to remember is: A positive presenter is a person who says what they think and feels what they say. This is the route to being truly inspirational, a person who completely *embodies* their message. Presentation means:

Noun	Giving a "present"
Adjective	Being "present" in the moment
Verb	Doing the "present"-ing

From this we see that "presentation" is mostly about giving a "present" when we are "present" or "pre-sent!"

It is great fun to give gifts! In our society, we traditionally organize special occasions on which to formally give gifts: birthdays, christenings, weddings, Christmas, or other religious festivals. And for the giving of gifts to be joyful, we give what the person wants and what we want to give—what we want them to have enjoyment of. Public speaking is the same. Give your audience what they want and what you want to give. When public speaking situations are full of panic or havoc, it is always because the speaker is not "present" and, therefore, does not see or sense the audience or the space. When we become "non-present," we are unaware of living in the moment, and through tension push ourselves to the point of finishing, which is filled with tension. This is the consequence of being self-conscious, rather than self-aware; there is a big difference between the two states.

Self-consciousness means a state of only being conscious of self, to the exclusion of everyone and everything else. When self-consciousness exists there is no sense of the individual enjoying the "gift" of the situation, and most physical behavior or body language becomes "non-present." When communication processes are not "embodied," the delivery of information occurs from a "talking head," as opposed to a "body voice." This means the individual is not tuned to their signature note as a consequence of the tensions that flood through their physical being. By contrast, when the individual is "present," they are self-aware, meaning aware of self in relation to the moment and the situation, and clearly sensing the energy of those in the surrounding space.

My belief is that the only way we can be effective public speakers is if we experience contact with the entirety of ourselves—physically, emotionally, mentally, and spiritually—creating full self-awareness and the ability to be fully present. Then we create and radiate a feeling of being Calm, Commanding, and Conscious, as well as Healthy, Wealthy, and Wise. From this state of being, if your intention is precise, you will engender a personality full of presence, gravitas, charisma, magnetism, and star quality. When every cell in your body vibrates with intending and attending, you achieve the phenomenon I referred to in Chapter 3, known by professional athletes as being in "the zone."

Scientifically, this state is closely akin to the brain sine wave known as Alpha, in which both hemispheres of the brain connect and produce "otherworldly" feelings of limitless potential. In short, the race runs you rather than you running the race, and can only be achieved by "owning" self and operating from a state of rest rather than from a point of tension.

Creating Rapport

When speaking in public, whatever the size of the audience, whether it be small or large, my experience suggests that very few people prepare themselves adequately for the mass energy they will experience from the attention of the onlookers. To present successfully, we must expand our energy focus and the dimensional field of our operation—in short, think big and your energy field will expand. In this way, you will begin to create a sense of rapport between you and your audience.

The energy of the audience is almost always positive—audiences want to be there, otherwise they wouldn't have come. They want to be enlightened, entertained, and informed; they would much rather the event were a success than a failure. Most audiences only alienate the speaker when they feel alienated by the speaker. So set out with the belief that the audience is a friend, on your side, not a foe to be tamed, persuaded, or overcome. This is why I do not believe it is useful to imagine the audience is sitting in front of you completely naked, as some presentation consultants suggest. This is to the detriment and disempowerment of others. Far better simply to smile at a room full of friends. It can work wonders.

So many of the public speakers I consult do not prepare by visualizing their audience before the event. Work out the following:

- How will it feel to stand before X number of people?
- Where should I stand for best advantage? (This is something I refer to as "Power Spotting" or "Anchoring.")
- What can I do to create maximum impact on X number of people?
- An aligned spine and an alive physicality always communicates confidence. What is your body doing/being?

In order to fully captivate your audience, you must attempt to visit the auditorium, room, or building in which you will speak before the day or time of your presentation. This will prepare and empower you for the size of the audience and the space, the advantages and disadvantages. You will be able to visualize how people will be positioned, choose your "power-spot" and how best to move, choose whether or not you will have a lectern or table, how the space is illuminated, and what amplification is needed. In effect, you will be able to choose how to have the biggest impact on your audience.

Remember to always check the ambience or atmosphere of the space. Will your audience be alive with attention sitting where they are placed? List all the commonsense considerations that are important to you, and this will safeguard you, making the presentation one of definite and perhaps even infinite success.

It is also important to recognize that the audience wants a two-way communication, rather than to be spoken "at" or preached to, as the following example illustrates only too well.

> Several years ago, I was approached by a well-known politician, Mr B, a specialist in industrial relations. I was helping him to prepare and deliver a speech during a time of political challenge, when his role as a communicator was a priority. Mr B could engineer relationships with great aplomb on the industrial platform and was a keen debater. However, on this occasion something went wrong.
>
> The speech was well written and well prepared, but the audience was rowdy. Halfway through the speech, one couldn't hear Mr B because of a yelling faction within the crowd. Mr B continued to try his best until debris was thrown at the podium, at which point he was immediately whisked off the platform by officials. I was waiting backstage and suggested that the audience was rowdy because people felt they were not being heard; their trials and tribulations were not being honored, and so they were feeling alienated.
>
> Mr B went back onto the platform and asked the audience to quieten so that he could hear questions. After a while a genuinely authentic conversation started, through which Mr B was able to answer those members of the audience who felt they were being ignored. Within a short passage of time, the audience calmed down, so that the evening ended on a successful note. At the beginning, Mr B was presenting information at the audience rather than speaking to them. They felt alienated and responded aggressively. As soon as Mr B took notice of what they had to say and empathized with their concerns, he became a friend, and they were engaged.

The best way to approach an audience and to develop rapport is to imagine you are simply having a conversation, and that the conversation, and the energy behind it, is the same conversation you would have with your family at home. For example, visualize a conversation you might have over breakfast or at dinner, when rapport is easily established and the energy flow is lively. Then relive the same force with your audience.

Developing rapport is a very sensual activity, almost like making love. You are hopefully relaxed, fully sensing, and aware of each aspect of joy that you wish your partner to be thrilled by. When this ceases, lovemaking ceases!

Speak to a hundred people as though you were speaking to one person, making sure that full eye contact is made as you scan the audience, so that you create easy, free-flowing, focused contact with different areas of your audience. If a sense of connection is alive in your delivery, your audience will feel that they are being talked to, not being talked at and consequently patronized. Assess your vocal tone, live in your signature note; don't shout—it never works.

Audience Techniques

Sometimes audiences can be hard work and need to be won over. In these situations, keep a cool head and live in the moment. A difficult audience will be impressed if you can create a sense of presence and command their attention, and it is worth bearing in mind that when you wish to do this, silence can be very effective—less is always more!

> On one occasion I worked with Sarah, a young bilingual sales manager, who was preparing a presentation for French business operatives. The style of presentation in French business is often confrontational, and Sarah was nervous after a previous experience when the majority of the audience brought out newspapers to read during her presentation.
>
> I prepared her by suggesting that if she were to experience a similar situation, she should wait in silence until the audience members were once more focused on her, and then ask them if there was any other data they would prefer.
>
> After the event Sarah told me that the audience had, indeed, brought out their newspapers again. Although she was very nervous, Sarah waited in silence. Gradually those holding newspapers noticed what was happening and put away what they were reading. At this point, conversation rather than confrontation began, and Sarah was able to give her presentation effectively, and with the gift of success that was rightly hers to own.

Riding the Tiger

When rapport is established with an audience, the energy field of the body expands to accommodate the broadened focus of energy coming toward you. Feelings are intensified, rhythms are enhanced, body language is magnified, and vocal delivery is amplified. This is something I call being in touch with "the tiger." The tiger is an amalgam of our insecurities or the voice of the inner critic, which often tells us we are not good enough. If we can "ride the tiger," then the tiger does not ride us. If the "tiger rides us," our tempo or rhythm moves too swiftly, we become "non-present," we do not focus, and we simply talk "at" our audience rather than "to" them.

Body Architecture

The following exercise will enable you to discover within yourself a truly inspirational mode of being. It will help you to align your spine, and this always communicates and creates power and confidence, because with the spine in alignment we are in balance. Use the exercise before presentation situations to create calm, to be focused, and to stay wholly present.

1. Find a space in which you can stand with ease. It is important that your energy field should not feel "contracted" by other people or pieces of furniture being too close to you. Move if you need to.
2. Begin to align your spine by placing your feet parallel, with your body weight balanced over the ball and heel of each foot, through the instep. We often stand with our weight solely on our heels, and as a consequence we unbalance our body's center of gravity, which is within the sacrum in the base of the spine. If we stand with the weight back, when we move forward we hold our body weight back, with our head in the past, rather than forward in the future. This signals that we live our lives "retroactively" rather than "proactively."
3. Next, imagine that you have roots growing from your feet and moving into Mother Earth. If you prefer, see these roots as columns of light force moving into the very structure of the earth. This "rootedness" will give you a sense of really being in connection with gravity and will give you confidence and power. Check that your knees are not locked; if we lock our knees we become rigid in our movement and block the potential flow of physical energy. If this "lock" occurs, you will always feel your voice to be tense.
4. Now tuck your pelvis slightly under. Try not to do this by tensing your buttocks, but rather by stroking your hands from the lower back over your bottom. Notice how this encourages an easy length in the lower part of your spine, with a firmness occurring in your lower abdomen. This will allow you to feel very supported.

5. From this position, lengthen or align your spine upward, as though it were a column of light. Try not to push forward but feel the length of your spinal light growing from your tailbone through your back and eventually along the length of your neck.

6. If your shoulders feel tense, lift them to your ears, tense them slightly, then let them go, so that they hang easily, like a coat hanger, from your upper body. Check that your shoulders are not rounded or braced back, otherwise you will feel tense and constricted. Now make sure your heart chakra is open and wide, just like the shoulder blade area.

7. If you look at yourself in profile in a full-length mirror, you will see your shoulder over your hip and your hip over the center of your foot. This may feel unusual, but remember that we are moving your body alignment into a form of Body Architecture that is completely "natural," even though, because of the bad postural habits we all develop as we grow up, it may not be familiar to you.

8. Now imagine that your spine is filled with a light force, like a laser beam. Imagine the shaft of the laser penetrating the floor beneath your feet and zooming downward through the strata into the very womb of Mother Earth. Perhaps the roots you created earlier are still functioning, so blend the imagery to help you feel even more alive, rich, and enlightened. Then bring the light laser up through the strata and back into your body, then through your spine, seeing the light even brighter than before and fueled by Mother Earth's natural force. Take the laser right through your spine and out into the atmosphere above your head. See it traveling through the stratosphere, and eventually let it go off into the mysteries of the universe.

9. Breathe a light-filled breath through the whole of your spine. Breath is inspiration!

10. Sound "*AH*" right through the position of your signature note. You may need to repeat this several times with your eyes open or closed, and eventually you will feel filled with light, color, and sound. Bathe in the fullness of your voice, feeling the resonance as light filling the whole of your physical geometry. Check that the position of your head is balanced with a long neck to achieve this. Try to keep your throat open, with

a relaxed jaw and released "tongue root"; use the *"GEE, GEE, GEE"* practice (see page 38), if you feel your throat is closed. This will prevent the resonance from sounding metallic.

10. When complete, pause for a moment and close your eyes. Listen into a distant sound and still any "mind-chatter." Then imagine the whole of your skin is a sheath around your being, full of the light of your breath force and protecting the "inner kingdom" of you from "outer world disturbance." Feel yourself literally "soaking in your own truth." The skin is our body's largest organ—see this sheath filled with the light focus of your five senses: *feel, hear, smell, taste,* then open your eyes and really *see.*

11. Notice how present you feel. Everything will appear brighter, clearer, more alive. This will allow you to be and feel full of presence and open-heartedly capable of charisma—one who is filled with charity and grace and light. You will be a magnetic focus and reference for your audience.

Inspirational speakers are filled with this breath/light force; they are literally "on fire" with the persona, passion, and presence that informs the space and the audience around them. Practice this exercise regularly, and use it before every presentation and you, too, will be filled with inspiration and presence.

In Conclusion…

The man that hath no music in himself,
Nor is not moved with concord of sweet sounds,
Is fit for treasons, stratagems and spoils;
The motions of his spirit are dull as night,
And his affections dark as Erebus:
Let no such man be trusted.

My interpretation of this is that if we are in tune with our signature note, we are in harmony with a concord of sweet sounds. Our integrity, our probity, and our purity fills the quality of our speaking. For the Renaissance speaker this was largely a question of a code of honor that permeated society and was the essence of the noble mind. What was the point of abusing the privilege of influence with falsehood? This meant one could not be trusted and, therefore, a lack of faith would occur. In the age of the spin-doctor, at the beginning of the twenty-first century, we are all far too aware of the deleterious effect of misinformation.

The inspirational speaker is full of the harmony, the concord of sweet sound, and, therefore, the delivery is sensational. An audience always responds through its mind and body, opening up with generosity and joy. This in turn leads to synergy, rapport, and infinite intelligence.

CHAPTER 10

†HE POWER †O †RAΠSMVTE

If you ask me what I came into the world to do I will tell you;
I came to live out loud.

—*PROUST*

The observations of life, the practical exercises and the work formats within this book arise from one central belief: sound is at the core of creation. This is the force that brought the universe alive.

An Eastern belief is that the word *universe* means "one sound" or Shabd, while Christian belief suggests that, "In the beginning was the Word, and the Word was with God, and the Word was God."

While studying Aramaic (the language of Christ) and early Christian writing in the Vatican library, the philologist and archeologist Professor Edmond Szekely came upon mysterious Aramaic texts. These texts dated from the third century A.D., and in one document entitled "The Essene Gospel of Peace," he found a transcript that read: "In the beginning was the Sound, and the Sound was with God, and the Sound was God."

The early Greek scribes who notated the Synoptic Gospels used the Greek word *Logos* for sound, which through the ages became translated into "the Word." As we have seen, *Logos* is the aspect of ancient Greek philosophy that quantifies cosmic reason, and its function is as the source of world order and intelligibility through speech or sound, with which we measure the qualities of knowing the universe. So if sound can create a universe, move mountains, shatter walls, and create images from within the human body, what other miracles might it be capable of?

We live in a time of great change, in which we are racing to acquire power, information, and stimuli. So it's vital that we remember that our voices are the means by which to achieve the qualities we need, to create the life we truly want. Without the added dimension of our own signature note, our path forward will be made more complex, more challenging, and our gains will be experienced solely within what is rational, so that the magic of life will be suppressed. One of the magical possibilities is that we can cure imbalance and sickness using the power of sound. If we can achieve this, what other magic can be created? The answer is: whatever we choose. The power of sound can be applied by each of us to our own lives, so that we may transform ourselves physically, emotionally, mentally, and spiritually. We can shift negativities within the material and subtle energetic planes using the instrument of sound that each of us is born with: our own voice.

Now that you have discovered your signature note and opened up your voice to the awakening of its true potential, you will begin to see great effects in your daily life. If we truly feel the sound of our voice through the whole of our body we open ourselves to the richness of our being and the richness of the world—and creative manifestation is imminent!

In this, our final chapter, I will return to the notion I introduced at the beginning of the book. Just as the ancients believed that the sound of God's voice had the power to create, so our voices, when expanded and enriched, have the power to awaken the creative force within us. With this creative power fully awake and alert, we are able to release the unhappiness of the past and move forward, empowered and with the ability to transform ourselves and our lives.

Sound That Transmutes

As we have seen in many of the Books of Wisdom throughout our world, it is stated that matter may be creatively changed, transformed, or transmuted through the use of sound. Each one of us has the power to create, and this creative power can be awakened through the voice. As we learned to suppress our feelings while growing up, so we learned to suppress much of our original creativity. Many of us in our maturity experience material success, yet have no idea how creatively powerful we truly are. All we have to do to awaken this creative power is to take action.

To bring about creative change, we simply need to begin by defining the state or condition we wish to transform. The trouble is, many of us have profound difficulty recognizing what this state is in the first place. We become so outwardly focused that we lose touch with our inner sense of self and our inner awareness of what we need.

Now is the time for you to become conscious of those people or things that drain your energy reserves. I ask you to shift consciousness by deciding that you no longer wish to be connected with such negativity. Perhaps it may not be a person but an establishment, or a habit, or an addiction— they are all energy holdings.

All things are transmutable; all we need is the ability to locate the point of our disturbance, and then use will to change the energy or the landscape. Can we truly use will to take action and change what is unsatisfactory in our lives? Yes! Energy cannot be wasted, time cannot be wasted—two figures of speech used to describe our own reluctance to take action and change. Become "responsible" (meaning the ability to respond) not "irresponsible" (the lack of ability to respond). Change the aspect of your life you know you no longer require because it has become obsolete and no longer serves you. Once energy was drawn from the process of interacting with it, but this no longer works.

Through the laws of physics, we can see that energy constantly transforms itself, in a perpetual unfolding of creative evolution. It is only we human beings who wish to hold or fix our lives in a search for permanency, believing that if we find it all will be well. We call this security. Usually we attempt to bring security into our lives through possessions that provide us with a sense of reality through "status." For a short while we feel our ego is satisfied, until we realize that all is not well and dissatisfaction sets in again. Chasing after more possessions will not solve the problem. True SECURE-ITY means SELF-CURE and cannot be provided by some outer thing or human being. When our creative energy is totally led by the desire for material permanency, we fail to understand that all conditions are temporary, including life and death.

So how can we shift or transmute the negative ego attachments we have into the spiritual attitudes we want to create?

TRANSMUTATIONAL CREATIVITY EXERCISE

Consider the following, see how they apply to your own unique experience, and decide which is reality and which is illusion!

Ego Attachment	Spiritual Attitude
Fear	Love
Superiority	Equality
Competition	Cooperation
Problems	Challenges
Victim	Victor
Insecurity	Self-confidence
Judgment	Discernment
Guilt	Innocence
Negative Involvement	Positive Detachment
Pessimism	Optimism

Control	Empowerment
Dependency	Preference
Impatience	Patience
Reactive	Responsive
Sin	Mistake
Jealousy	Detachment
Self-punishing	Self-fulfilling
Rejection	Projection
Automatic Pilot	Conscious Creation
Indulgence	Balance
Alone	All One
Worry	Faith
Envy	Abundance
Poverty	Prosperity
Arrogance	Humility
Boredom	Enthusiasm
Conditional Love	Unconditional Love
Illusion	Truth
Despair	Hope
Martyrdom	Self-balance
Lessons	Gifts
Embarrassment	Feeling Free
Cursing	Blessing
Grudging	Forgiving
Impotency	Potency
Lazy	Discipline
Powerlessness	Self-mastery
Depression	Expression

It is my adamant belief that when we open ourselves to the fullness of our transmutational creativity, we truly connect with our personal power—to thine own self be true. As we connect with our personal power, we also connect with our signature note, our own unique vibration. This is when destiny reveals itself to us, so that we may live the life that fills us full of joy … this is the quality of experience that many of our ancestors believed was the very song of the soul.

Letting Go of the Past

To wholly move forward in our lives we must be able to let go of the past. All the influential voices we have heard during our lives are stored within our bodies at a cellular level. This is why hearing a voice, a piece of music, or even a familiar phrase from the past can evoke powerful memories.

Vocal energies can hold negative power over us. For example, we often carry around in our beings the unkind words and phrases others have uttered toward us in our past, and we replay them to ourselves like recordings or programs, inaccurately using them to justify our unhappiness or failure in certain areas of life.

During an Alchemy of Voice workshop in the United States, I met Phyllida, who had been a powerful principal at a progressive Ivy League private school in New England. Phyllida had had an extremely successful career as a leading educator, and although she was retired she still functioned in *ex officio* capacities, as well as sitting on the committees of several charities. Phyllida had never married, but lived her vocation to the full and had had successful intimate relationships. However, there was one area of her psyche that plagued or "niggled" her constantly, and that was the critical voice of her mother, which she carried with her in her head. This also appeared bodily through slight eczema on the back of each hand, which had appeared when her mother had died.

During an empowerment exercise toward the end of the workshop, I set up the possibility of each person receiving healing from the group. One of the options (which Phyllida elected) was to walk slowly through the circle while one's name was chanted or sounded.

We were a large group of around forty people, and so it was a large circle that Phyllida stepped into. She walked through the circle feeling fully held by the group, fully supported by their positivism and by their love. When she got to the center she suddenly collapsed to the floor and cried. In these situations crying or weeping is not unusual, and so we simply held Phyl in our chanting and loving, honoring her tears, which were a blessing and a rich healing, before I stepped forward to her.

I asked her if she could tell us what had happened. She told us that she had felt completely released by the exercises we had done during the day and had stepped into the circle feeling great joy, when to her utter amazement she heard the voice of her mother in her head (her mother had been dead for over twenty years): "Who do you think you are!" Phyl's mother had been extremely controlling, praise was rarely given, but criticism was lavished abundantly. This mother could not appreciate her daughter but was always full of disapprobation.

I asked Phyl to walk the circle again, so that we could help her transmute or alchemize her pain. I asked her to think and feel the opposite sensations from the original pain—to feel herself free, independent, detached, and full of joy. All the elder women in the group stepped forward (as archetypal witnesses, like the ancestral line), and we chanted with joy in our hearts, to release the pain Phyl had experienced.

We all laughed with Phyl as she flew across the room, not in any hurry, but because she felt compelled by the healing. She said it felt as though angels were carrying her over the seeming abyss, and the voice of her mother transmuted into permission, approbation, release, and love.

Three weeks later, she called me to say that there had been no recurrence of the eczema, and to tell me how she had remembered, after the workshop, her mother slapping her hands in early life whenever she had been out of order.

Obviously, not all our challenges are so fundamentally simple to release. But the fact remains that there is always the potential to grow and to transmute. Remember the universal truth: nothing happens that is random; all events are guided by a higher wisdom. Chaos is an illusion—there is total order in all events; we simply need to perceive it as such, even when an event is deeply shocking. Nothing happens without a reason; we simply need to find out what the reason is. In all activities, there is the possibility for change, for growth. The clarion call is: thought creates reality.

The remarkable book *Conversations with God* by Neale Donald Walsch provides us with an illustration concerning the cycle of evolution that illuminates the power of thought:

What you THINK you create,
What you CREATE you become,
What you BECOME you express,
What you EXPRESS you experience,
What you EXPERIENCE you are,
What you ARE you think,
What you THINK you create

Below is an exercise that will help you in the process of transmuting all that you wish to change in your life.

TRANSMUTATION VISUALIZATION

1. Begin by moving yourself to your sacred space and removing any unnecessary distractions.
2. In a sitting position, align your spine, checking that you are comfortably warm and cushioned.
3. Burn some incense and play your favourite CD of sacred music. Allow yourself to move from the daily *doing* into an energy of *being*—change vibration.
4. Close your eyes.
5. Bring the pranic force of breath through your spine as a conductor and see the energy moving down into the earth as well as soaring up into the heavens. Feel connected with Mother Earth and Father Heaven.
6. See the breath as a light force filling the whole of your being and sound "*Ah*" through your signature note, cleansing your energy field, and releasing any psychic debris that you may have picked up during your day.
7. Change the *Ah* to another sacred chant if you wish, such as the *Om*. This will allow you to fully align your energies and move into an Alpha state.
8. Be still and silent for a moment, observing, in detachment, any sensations, intimations, or intuitions that may occur.
9. In this fuller sense of your inner space, your inner kingdom will reveal what you know, or think, or feel you wish to transmute. Meditate on this for as much time as you need.
10. Visualize the force, the scenario, the sensations, or the memory that you wish to transmute. If, for some reason, you cannot discern what it is, simply remain within Silence, Solitude, and Stillness until you do. Focus into your heart—the heart is all-knowing when open, whereas your head will move you to polarities such as "Shall I, shan't I? Will I, won't I?"
11. See that which you wish to transform. Visualize all aspects of the process, and then move the force to a door visualization in your mind's eye. As you approach the door, feel it opening onto a landscape that will receive the force you wish to let go.
12. Let go of the force and close the door.
13. When the door has closed, blow all your breath at the door seven

times, and then reopen the door to see the force positioned in an opposite incarnation, transmuted, revealed, released.

14. All energy is transmutable, and so simply be with this notion, sending thanks and love to the universe through sounding *Ah*, before you finish the process by making sure all aspects of your energy are protected. To do this, visualize yourself surrounded by a white light, showered in gold—gold will insulate your energy, protecting you from any outer negativity.

Base Metal into Gold

When we fully discover our signature note and our personal power we discover our true potency, and this leads to potential alchemy.

The original alchemists believed their work to be illuminated by the Philosopher's Stone (an imaginary or real substance by which base metals were turned to gold, an early example of a catalytic agent), which transmuted the mundane into the Divine. This art arose from a noble lineage that came from the deep past of human experience on Earth.

The Egyptians believed that the God Thoth brought to Earth the divine knowledge of alchemy, alongside the philosophies of astrology and numerology. Thoth is often linked with Hermes, the Greek messenger of the Gods, and in Roman belief this God was Mercury. Thoth (or Hermes Trismegistus) gave mankind powerful teachings known as the Hermetic Teachings.

This is a statement said to be taken from a book that Thoth left for mankind known as the Kybalion:

> *The principles of truth are seven. He who knows these*
> *understandingly possesses the magic key before whose touch all*
> *doors of the temple will fly open. O people of Earth, men born and*
> *made of the elements and with the spirit of the divine within you,*
> *rise from your sleep of ignorance. Be sober and thoughtful.*
> *Realize that your home is not Earth, but in the Light.*

Alchemy teaches that God, the creative force, is within and without everything, He is one universal spirit manifesting in all forms reaching into infinity.

In the spiritual nature of man, this force functions through regeneration; in the material body, comprising of the elements, this force is known as transmutation. Thus, through alchemy, all souls and all minds realize a mutual kinship. This signifies that the highest aspiration is altruism, and this knowledge is capable of solving all of life's challenges.

The Renaissance thinkers believed that through the work of all pure art, as a process of learning, any mass of mental ignorance could be transmuted into wisdom. Renaissance thought saw man as the foremost creation of God. Within the nature of man is reflected the entire universe in miniature, as within each seed, each cell, each grain of sand, each drop of water is concealed all parts, aspects and elements of the cosmos. Therefore, alchemy was seen as the Art of Increasing; by its nature, it brings into full power the greatest and highest excellence.

Try the following "Sonic Alchemy" exercise to enrich your vibration.

1. Begin by moving to your sacred space and prepare by aligning the energies for a special task. Burn incense, transform the vibration by tuning into your favorite CD, burn candles (a candle's flame is one of the purest forces that reaches into infinity).

2. Align your spine and relax by tuning into the light of your breath, reaching down into Mother Earth and soaring into Father Heaven.

3. Open each chakra by visualizing the color of each "wheel" turning in a clockwise direction—simply breathe each chakra into creation, spinning its own glory.

4. Meditate on what you most wish to create. Tune into your heart to truly discern the nature of this. The desire that accompanies this creation will enliven its manifestation.

5. Chant Ah through your heart chakra, having found your note, and in its own increasing develop the Ah into Om or Namaha (the mother of mantras). See your heart turn into a beautiful ball of light.

6. Be still for a moment, and observe any negative currents that may disturb your chanting. Simply let all debris release itself into the ether through the power of thought.

7. Visualize yourself sitting in a golden pyramid, and again tune into the sonic chant that you feel most empowers you in this moment. Feel yourself in one unified field of light within, through, and around your whole body.

8. See the Alpha energy of your being seven inches above your head, and the Omega energy seven inches below your body within the golden pyramid. This begins to open you fully to the light vehicle that you are.

9. Visualize the whole unified field of light connecting with the light of the universe.
10. Chant *Om Namaha Shivaya* and see your light vehicle connecting with the presence of the source.
11. Feel the highest level of your spirit (your Higher Self) radiating forth into the universe and transforming the whole of your consciousness into pure light.
12. Draw the pranic cord of light up from Mother Earth and the ground into the vastness of your spirit within your golden pyramid.
13. Visualize another pyramid opening above your own, on this occasion reversed as in a mirror. You are now connecting with the parallel realities of the planet's hologram.
14. Allow the teachings to pour into your heart chakra at the center of the unified light, and then be still.
15. When you wish to finish, simply sound *Om*, and withdraw the energies from the dual aspect of the pyramidic consciousness, eventually closing down each chakra.
16. Complete by sitting in stillness, and simply be.

This is an incandescent "Sonic Alchemy." It will allow you to feel bathed in the harmonics of the universe.

In Conclusion...

Our daily lives are often so overwhelmed by the pressures and strains of modern life that we are left exhausted, functioning only on a superficial level. This book is a call to you to shift, re-create, and transmute the negative into the positive.

By discovering your signature note and the power you have to transform anything you wish to change in your life, you are enriching and expanding your horizons. Instead of being tied or overwhelmed by the pressures and limitations of daily life, you have the potential to remove such obstacles and spread your wings, flying as high as you wish.

Your voice is the key to change, to healing, to expansion, and to personal power. Develop a voice that is truly yours, a voice that conveys to others your depths and abilities, and discover where it will take you. Never again settle for a voice mask—a voice that is shaped or confined by others and that does not truly represent you. Never suppress or limit the power of your voice to "fit in" with others.

Your true voice, carried on the wings of your breath, is all you need to begin transforming your life. Shape your life by using your signature note. It is the master key that will unlock the future you choose—a future filled with joy, energy, happiness, and success.

The Voice In The Fire

The time has come to turn your heart
Into a Temple of Fire.
Your sound is gold hidden in the dust
To reveal its splendor
You need to burn in the fire of love.
—RUMI

It has been five extraordinary years since *The Alchemy of Voice* was first published, and much has happened to expand the profound experience of its healing process. The evolving cycle of Sound Healing workshops, many public appearances, and one-to-one Soul Readings have connected me with a wider audience and brought me great satisfaction. The heartfelt support and nourishment from many wonderful people all over the globe who have passed through the portal of the work have enriched my life. They have encouraged me with the kind of love that burns golden in the fire.

I have continued to undergo many initiations during this process, for the deeper we travel on the mystical pathway, the more we are challenged to broadly open our hearts on our journey toward the Divine Mother and Father. We must prise open every part of our being, clearing away the dashing courage of the ego, and yielding to the simplicity of love and compassion.

The journey has been greatly assisted by the enchantments of my unseen guides the archangels, particularly Archangel Michael. I have been deeply moved and humbled by the profound lessons received from these enchanting companions. At times, great searing pain has accompanied the mystical pathway opening up in front of me. But then, just as I imagined that my way forward was emotionally polluted, I've felt the elation of veneration as I glimpsed the great gatekeepers of Awe and Joy. These gatekeepers sanctify the entrance to the Temple of Fire, for they stand by the sacred spot where the Love Gold lies, deep in the dust of the ashes. With them watching over me, in an instant, my spirit has turned from fear and pain to adoration and deep love.

The body of work contained in *The Alchemy of Voice* may be understood as in ancient times, as a Temple of Healing. Such temples originated in ancient Atlantis and Egypt, where the intelligence and compassion of the heart, moved by the vibration of the soul's note, brought great harmonic power to the people. Sound and its myriad resonances, like sparkling light from crystal, connected the faithful, time and time again, with the prize that was above all other: to be with the Divine.

The Alchemy of Voice was revealed to me through an evolving series of twelve "works" that constitute the Temple of Healing. At present, only seven works exist; more will follow, as we evolve on a cellular level. The "works" were designed by twelve archangelic beings who first gave me the enchantment of the work. They inspire us to proclaim acts of deep-hearted love through sacred voice. Alchemy offers the gift of transmutation healing, pranic upliftment, and spiritual empowerment. It defines us crucially and unequivocally.

The objective of the work is designed in such a way as to change us from a dispersed fear-based culture to an interconnected love-based collective, so as to make the largest soul-stride possible at this time of remarkable change. Make no mistake: even as we watch the death of a world we once knew, we are also observing the birth of a Golden Aquarian Age.

Our midwife is Sound. Through its power, we are born, mature, and fulfil our destiny and through our unique essence. Our entire cellular being is involved—physically, emotionally, mentally, and spiritually. This experience offers us the possibility of living as "human angels," here in the earthly realm, utterly changed by the chord of the sacred sound that heralded creation.

Mahatma Gandhi said: "Be the change you want to see in the world." The "works" are one pathway we may choose to become that change—not as a possibility but living the probability of radical embodiment by which the word is made flesh, full of grace and truth. *The Alchemy of Voice* (also often known as Voice Alchemy) is deeply concerned with the harmonics of transmutation, through which we have the opportunity to soak deeper and deeper in the sacred soul of sound—to feel the holy instant of sound vibrating deep within our physical membrane, with a weight and conviction that moves mountains.

This harmonious vibration is vast and potent, for it unifies mind, body, and soul. Harmony is benign yet powerful; through it, we achieve a unique fusion of embodiment and spiritual integration. Just as the alchemists of old intended, the embodied divine human is the "philosopher's stone." When we emerge suffused with divine love, we discover the "stone" multiplies to infinity, endlessly repeating as we use breath-light and sound. We become selfless instruments of the divine, moving like thousands of meteors throughout the cosmos.

Initially, as we begin working with *The Alchemy of Voice*, we find that the "works" offer a way of rediscovering our "signature note," the song of our soul, a means of finding our core power by transmuting those behaviors that have stopped us from being the people we want to be. As we achieve harmony, we begin to live our true power, and this is our celestial sovereignty living in a passionate engagement with compassion. So, we reclaim the kingdom of our soul's joy and become once more conscious of our link with the *I AM* presence—the monad, or source-filled soul group, from whence we came. This means that we are able to truly evolve as star beings, using the vibration of love to perpetrate acts of eternal joy.

I first received the "works" from twelve brilliant archangels during a meditation at Glastonbury Tor on August 17, 1987. Then, further visitations from these angelic messengers occurred throughout the following year, which assisted me in processing the information I was receiving.

It is difficult to put into words what it felt like to experience the images and teachings I was given by these supernal fifth-dimensional Matrix Teachers. It came in the form of a series of enchantments, both an agony and an ecstasy, far surpassing anything I had ever experienced before. The agony felt like a sword of light piercing deeper and deeper into my chest, whereas the ecstasy filled my heart with gratitude that I had been considered worthy of the initiation, to carry forth a knowledge that would inspire the love of many, kindling the fire in the heart of our sound. Harmonics of fantastic proportion and waves of fluorescent force dashed through me, accompanying the images and teachings. The spiraling force moved me at once to rapture, and then to despair.

My mind raced with questions. How could I be the proportion of light that was indicated? How could I carry out the task, with all my failings, with all my mistakes and corruptions? At one point, I remember feeling not thwarted and diminished but angry and enraged that this was something I was being asked to do. Was sacrifice required of me? I had undergone two prior "dark night of the soul" experiences that had wracked the very bedrock of my nerves. Was this my lot again? Was I ready?

It then came to me that my task on this occasion was not to be achieved through sacrifice but through my soul gladly relinquishing itself to the rite of service. Feelings cascaded through me as I felt both felled and free, and as I looked into the ether, in a feeble attempt to gather myself, I was shown the source of the teachings: a gargantuan cache of "original thought." Deep voices penetrated the very fiber of my psyche with the knowledge that this information arose from the cosmic computer of the Akashic Records—a hall of memory for every thought, a compendium of mystical knowledge encoded in the seventh dimension, a nonphysical plane of existence.

I saw what looked like two spiral staircases, instantly reminding me of visionary artist-poet William Blake's painting of Jacob's Ladder; yet, on this occasion I was told these represented human DNA. Visions accompanied this radiance, with flashing scenes of what will be, and what has passed. There were images of Atlantis and Egypt mixed with future life, many of which were cataclysmic. Out of these chthonic wastelands grew islands of knowledge, which revealed to me that as each human being evolved, we would have the opportunity to radically embody divine grace and truth and create a kingdom of spirit on Earth.

Through a sound akin to a rushing mighty wind, I then heard a seraphic chorus giving voice to the elements of human transformation that may occur. I was told that humanity would live in the golden light of a new world filled with the fire of unconditional love, joy, and heartfelt passion. Each institution—financial, governmental, medical, religious, and educational—would smolder in the burning fire of the soul's smithy, and Earth People would be forged on the anvil of love, justice, and cooperation.

All of this and more left me dazed and exalted. The effect of these enchantments took me many weeks to process, and radically changed my world view. Everything had to change, including my partner of many years, who was utterly perplexed and simply couldn't accept or rationalize what had happened to me. This created a huge, irrevocable impasse between us that neither of us could surmount. I felt a strange mixture of bewilderment and resolution. I gave myself to the teachings with the only feelings I could dredge from my soul: my love, my faith, my hope, and my will.

August 15–17, 1987 is now recognized as a remarkable passage of time on Planet Earth and a unique time to be alive. Known as the Harmonic Convergence, it was a period when many oracles spoke forth their prophecy. A vast portal of energy revealed itself through a unique astronomical alignment, alerting our consciousness to a period of unprecedented change. This event, and the attendant changes to our physical and psychic lives, took place as a result of the sun and moon moving into direct alignment with six out of nine of our solar system planets, creating the form of a grand trine in the heavens: the planets were literally aligned at the apexes of an equilateral triangle. This began a period of accelerated development that would lead to a further astrological shifting point, twenty-five years later, on December 21, 2012. Currently, Planet Earth is feeling the intensification of accelerated spiritual growth and its attendant opportunity for enlightened social, economic, and political change.

Thousands of years ago, Mayan astronomers gave prophesy that a period of planetary quickening would occur between the Harmonic Convergence and December 21, 2012, the day when Earth will complete its 26,000-year orbital cycle around the sun. On this day of Winter Solstice there will be an alignment of all the planets within the solar system.

However, before this could be, Mayan Prophecy foretold that 144,000 Rainbow Light Warriors would be initiated as a consequence of the Harmonic Convergence, and would be made ready to prepare the way of the change. These human beings were soul-destined to bring forth teachings of love and peace to the people of Planet Earth through acts of great humility and dignity. Witnessing the endeavor of this compassion, other human beings would be encouraged and inspired to believe in their own immortality, to see that the whole of life is interconnected, and to live their lives through love as a pathway for conscious living.

"Conscious living" refers to a life filled with the illumination of soul consciousness, not a life consumed by the whisperings of linear history, much of which has incarcerated us in paradigms of thought formulated through countless illusions.

When we live consciously, we are inspired, moment to moment, by the truth that we are free spiritual beings making a human journey. When consciously living we realize the sole reason we chose to be incarnated is to create and joyously expand through love; anything else is an illusion. When we live consciously, we become present to the reality that, in essence, the whole of life is "flow," and that we must yield to the source to be directed to our heart's greatest desire. When we live consciously, we may come to the realization that we are protected by wise guides, some of angelic countenance. These beings of light have lovingly looked after us through eons of time, and yet they will only assist us when we ask. Wherever we are and whatever we are doing, our angelic and spirit guardians are enveloping us with eternal love, empathy, and compassion.

Surrounded by the embrace of the angels and enveloped by their love, we begin to awaken from the veil of amnesia that has hung like a miasma around our soul. We are brought to a place of bliss—a peace that passes all understanding. In this gentle way, our heritage is brought forward to meet our present. It was specifically created at source for us to live in our future. In the end, though, there is only the moment—when past, present, and future cease to exist as a temporal space and we achieve Oneness, or Unity.

During my archangelic instruction on Glastonbury Tor, the twelve archangels told me that we are beings of sacred life who merely touch the temporal domain. Through our very human existence, we serve as interpreters of the world of matter. The angels gave great treasure, reminding us all that sound is at the core of creation and our major form of transmutation. The angels are aware that we are losing sight of the soul's "songlines" in our traditions and cultures, and how we have learned power from them in the past. They helped create the "temple works" of *The Alchemy of Voice* to reconnect us with the source of these trajectories: by learning the chants of the *logos* and the mantra of sound existing around the great *OM*, and thereby we will download into the hardware of our DNA the software of the unified field of light.

In the past, our ancestral lines were kept open through the stories of oral history that we spoke or sang praising the divine. The experience of hearing the stories of old spoken out loud kept our memories clear, defined the old ways, taught us powerful truths for new ways of being, and strengthened or furbished our contact with the Essence. When the stories were told around the fire, we listened in amazement and memorized them from the keepers of stories among the elders. In this way, the tales of yore were kept alive in our bodies, particularly when ritualized around the great rhythmic cycles of the natural world, such as the Equinox and Solstice. These ceremonies of light and dark were maintained in reverence of the heavens, the sacred rulers of the Old World.

The people of those times vividly noticed what was occurring in the skies, as they often slept under the heavens during the warm seasons and only sought refuge in their huts, houses, and castles during the colder seasons. The stars and planets in the skies and heavens intrigued them. Telling stories kept alive the memories of old, the rhythms and cadences of their original language and telling, through oral traditions or recorded visually in carved petroglyphs, painted pictographs, or on old parchments. No matter where the stories came from, or how they were recorded, they all pointed in the same direction: man's place in the heavens. Watching the heavens was the Internet and entertainment of that time. Those who could translate the activities of the sky, the archeoastronomer-priests, were considered to be powerful oracles—intermediaries between the Heavenly Father and Mother (the Stellar Parents) and their terrestrial children.

During the latter part of the sixteenth century, great social change occurred, which produced a renaissance in the nature of our oral traditions. A relatively new invention—the printing press—led to a steady rise in publications of the printed word and literacy. Storytelling now became a formalized activity, particularly within Elizabethan playhouses.

Queen Elizabeth I's reign saw vast development in trade, an expanding political geography overseas, and the advancement of early modern science. These events put pressure on Elizabethan society and stretched European social parameters to breaking point. As a result, many of the oral traditions began to transform into formal entertainment. The life and love of the word-sound mostly was mostly alive in the playhouse, the pulpit, and the debating chamber. Words were kept alive in people's bodies as they participated as lively interactive audiences experiencing on a physical level the richness and vulgarity of the plays. This form of sharing the spoken word thrived until the act that closed the theaters in 1642 under Puritan reform.

During the Elizabethan/Jacobean era, speech came to be viewed and fabled as "decorated silence." Diaries from the period report that noble people were taught to speak eloquently, through an understanding of poetic rhythm; the acquisition of languages such as Latin, French, and Greek; and the harmonies of musical form. We know that Queen Elizabeth 1 spoke five languages fluently, danced a Galliard or two before breakfast (in full Farthingale, the dress of the time), and was particularly adverse to slovenly speech, for she once lamented the fact that she couldn't comprehend Sir Walter Raleigh's rough Devonshire accent.

Above all it was believed that speech was created by God to inspire and inform through "ambrosia speech"—or what we subsequently know as mellifluous, literally "honeyed," speech. The substance of every word was considered to be an emanation of political and religious efficacy, whereas the aesthetics of harmony was considered to be in direct proportion to the flow of bliss from the divine.

What has stopped us today from living lives of bliss? Why do we no longer experience ourselves as part of a vast sea of eternal awareness lapping the shores of our souls? What has moved us away from feeling at one with the force that flows throughout the cosmos? Why do we no longer experience the resonance of universal creativity?

We have experienced a series of devastating losses. Over the centuries, our deeply felt connection with Mother Earth, or Mother Divine, has been gradually replaced by scientific advances, the developments of the industrial revolution, and the increased function or preponderance of technology. All have led us to one place: NOISE. Noise of machines. Noise of our mental-chatter spawned by doing, doing, doing. Noise of our disconnection from the natural world. Noise of the many voices of fear lurking within. Noise of our daily anxiety. Noise of other people shouting in crowded social contexts. Noise of muzak. Noise of giving our power away. Noise of the toxicity we unwittingly place within our physical being. Noise of the pervasive electromagnetic static emanating from the tools of our living and the environment in which we place ourselves. Noise, noise, noise.

The effects of "noise" pollute and confuse our bodies and our lives until they break with impurity. As a result, it is crisis as a doorkeeper—not Christos—that opens the way to a more healthy series of choices. Finally, we heed the sound deep in our hearts. It is a note that may be initially contorted with pain; yet, because it is yearning to be heard, it quickly grows into something magnificent, a force to be reckoned with.

By using *The Alchemy of Voice*, we gradually quieten, distill, and transmute the noise of this internal combustion and counterbalance the ego's drive for more and more information, all of it designed to make us feel us feel more special, more exclusive. Within the lofty but lonely turret of the head, there is only the argument of competition driven by ego; whereas, when we lie in the compassion of the heart, we discover an oasis of love, truth, and purity.

Pre-Raphaelite artist Edward Burne-Jones said, "When they make another machine I will paint another Angel!" Visionary nineteenth-century poet Walt Whitman extolled the virtues of divine sound, raising the intuitive voice of the poet as a caveat against machines that drove forward the industrial revolution. Walt Whitman spoke loudly through the paeans of his own métier, urging our voices to embrace the divine (*Leaves of Grass*, 1891):

Vocalism, measure, concentration, determination and the Divine power to speak words;
Are you full-lunged and limber-lipped from long trial?
From vigorous practice? From physique?
Do you move in those broad lands as broad as they?
Come duly to the divine power to speak words?
For only at last after many years, after chastity, friendship, procreation, prudence and nakedness,
After treading ground and breasting river and lake,
After a loosened throat, after absorbing eras, temperaments, races,
After knowledge, freedom, crimes,
After complete faith, after clarifyings, elevations and removing obstructions,
After these and more, it is just possible there comes to a man, a woman, the divine power to speak words;
Then toward that man or woman swiftly hasten all—none refuse, all attend.

O what is it in me that makes me tremble so at voices?
Surely whoever speaks to me in the right voice, him or her I shall fol-
low, as the water follows the moon, silently, with fluid steps, anywhere
around the globe.

All wait for the right voices;
Where is the practiced and perfect organ? Where is the developed soul?
For I see every word uttered thence has a deeper, sweeter, newer sound,
impossible on lesser terms.

The Alchemy of Voice, in its very essence, brings coherence to mind, body, and spirit. Like the "philosopher's stone," sound functions as an instrument to help turn profane materia into spiritual gold. In order to fulfill our birthright and transform ourselves into beings of love, to make our dreams come true, to truly become receptive for the word to be made flesh, we must first go to the unseen world—the world of spirit, the divine, the place of inspiration. This is the crystal land where our imaginations are nourished, from which sound arises guiding us to a notion of the treasure we wish to create in our lives.

Diamond Sonic Meditation

Find yourself in a space where you feel the energies are harmonized and that you regard as sacred. This may be a room in your home, a dell in Mother Nature, or a niche in a natural landscape that moves your spirit deeply. If you have a designated meditation room in your home, please use that.

Light a candle, place a clear quartz crystal near you, play appropriate ambient music softly in the background, and burn incense, preferably frankincense, a powerful astral cleansing agent. These four measures will exquisitely purify the energy of your space and your field, and will significantly assist the transformational process you are about to engage in. Moreover, preparing in this way sends forth an intention into the cosmos that you wish to move into that exquisite, supernal chamber of consciousness where we meet the love of the divine.

Switch on voicemail and please turn off your computer. Simply inform any member of your household that you need Silence, Solitude, and Stillness.

Sit comfortably, feeling your body earthed or grounded. This may be cross-legged on the floor, or seated on a chair. Choose a position that allows you to feel in an optimized state to receive the exquisite angelic force.

Feel your spine aligned, and place your hands comfortably in your lap. You may want to use a *mudra*, a hand or finger gesture symbol that aligns sacred physical and metaphysical energies with your body. For example, if you bring the tip of your thumb and forefinger together you will feel a subtle connective tissue force aligning within. This mudra brings a connection between the moon and sun in your being, which means that both lunar and solar energies will be channeled through your present impulses. This aids a balance of yin and yang energies.

Release the breath from your body by breathing out, and smoothly take three deep breaths in and out of your body to release tension and toxins. Three is the number vibration of transformation, and so signals "consciousness" to prepare for change.

Feel the breath as light, the sacred *prana* fill each cell, allowing the breath to move wide and deep through your body. When complete pause and soak for a moment in this finely tuned state of awareness. When drenched in this state we are on the threshold of a hugely transformative portal.

Our sound work in this special sonic meditation is to open the eight chakras (seven internal and one outside the body), then use the Diamond Meditation given to us by Archangel Metatron. Metatron is the great teacher who shines through the geometry and essence of the clear diamond and the sister energy of the quartz crystal, for these are this angel's preferred elements.

These beautifully precious stones symbolize the powerful shining rays of God force on our planet. Diamonds are often created through the intense heat of a meteor colliding and fusing with carbon particles of the earth—such a fire is produced by this fusion, such an ecstasy of cosmic force meeting planetary terrain.

1. Imagine that you have a pure white laser light moving through your spine, this is your pranic cord. Visualize this light moving through the whole of your spine and down into the floor or chair upon which you sit. Draw the energy deeply into the building and earth's crust beneath you, and then visualize the cord moving through the soil, the clay, the stone, and rock. See the cord of light journeying deep into the magnetic core of our planetary home,

deep into the womb of Mother Earth, deep into the Earth Star of your own chakra system.

2. Pause for a moment, asking Mother Earth for a blessing, a symbol, or a sign, then draw or siphon the elixir of Her unconditional love upwards through the layers of the earth, through rock, stone, clay, and soil. Once you have drawn the intention and light up into your body, place Mother Nature's gift into the treasure of your heart's secret chamber, then allow the pranic cord to move upward and out through the top of your head. See it moving through the atmosphere of the planet and into the stratosphere. If you know your planetary idyll, or your celestial home beyond Planet Earth, go there, otherwise take the light of the pranic cord to the Planet Venus. This is the brightest star in the night's sky, the Planet of Love, from which the Goddess Aphrodite first came forth. Through her particular vibration, Venus graciously and lovingly watches over *The Alchemy of Voice*. Then return to your physical body here on Earth.

3. Check that your spine is still aligned and your body comfortable. Release any tension that may have occurred by letting go of your breath and then, in full response, inhale and draw breath deep into your body. Breathe it wide and deep, by opening your ribs, then your abdomen, rather than trying to "lift" the breath into your body, thereby creating tension in your upper chest or shoulders. Our work in this meditation is to feel how the elixir of sacred sound can be used for radical embodiment processes. This is challenging to achieve if we harbor tension. When we are tense we only give one small part of ourselves, whereas when we are relaxed we give of ourselves completely. So allow the breath to move throughout your being like the waves of circadian energy (the natural rhythms of our planet, like the movement of the tides). Remember to see the breath as nourishing white light moving through you. In a sense dropping into your interior, by moving the base of your ribs, and so breathing wide and then deep. Check you are not pushing the breath into your belly, which will also create tension.

4. Having checked you are free, once more see the vertical beauty of the pranic cord iridescently moving through you and beyond, like a vast column of laser light, connecting you with planetary and cosmic force. Then visualize a bright red disc, three inches in diameter, shining three inches beneath the base of your spine on

the cord. This is your root chakra. See the chakra surrounded by a diamond, within which we will place the sound of *AW*, spinning the chakra in a counterclockwise direction for the feminine energy, or clockwise for the masculine force. Do this three times. Breathe out, then in again. Once again breathe the *pranayama* all the way through you, imagining the breath as a light force filling the whole of your physical geometry.

5. Now move to the sexual identity center or sacrum, and imagine an orange wheel of light surrounded by a diamond three inches in diameter and sound *HOO* to move the chakra in a clockwise or counterclockwise direction. Do this three times, allowing the sound to move smoothly through the air about you and within you. If a jerking energy occurs in the breath, do not worry, simply let the breath diminish, take another breath, and begin again. Similarly, if you feel yourself beginning the sound with a harsh attack, let the energy go gently, rather than forcing it.

6. Now move to the solar plexus, which is just above your naval and yellow in color. Visualize a ball of light three inches in diameter within a diamond, and move it in either a clockwise or counterclockwise direction on the sound *HOH*. When you have completed this three times, pause and notice the powerful "earthing" energies that exude from your body as you electrify these consequential currents of force, the chakra centers of your biocomputer. For now, we move into the heart chakra and begin a different aspect of the meditation.

7. Move to the center of your sternum, where the heart chakra lies, and visualize a green wheel of light three inches in diameter inside a beautiful diamond. Sound *AH,* and move this wheel in either a clockwise or counterclockwise direction. Significant energies will move through you as we stimulate this database. Feel the love of the Source entering your body and producing a six-pointed star diamond around the green of your heart chakra. This is a radiantly powerful force as it marks a meeting point between Heaven and Earth and symbolizes the creation principle in two of the major wisdom traditions of our world: Judaism and Christianity. Similarly, in ancient Atlantis, it was believed that all numbers possess vibration. Number six was considered to be the number of the lovers—a joyous meeting of opposites, as above so below, like a sacred union of male and female!

8. Move to the throat center and visualize a blue wheel of light

within a diamond, three inches in diameter and moving in your appropriate direction. Then sound *HI,* which will open the center of self-expression in your being, and so feel your vibration extending off to embrace the planet, then beyond into the cosmos, feel your soul rippling through the beauty of your courageous voice out into the world and beyond, as well as it being anchored within. Feel the liberation of your absolute grace and truth, like waves moving through the ecstasy of your whole life and beyond into your future. Through this sound you will see the extent of your commitment to the textures and experiences of your life, warts and all. Simply let the joy of your soul extend itself out through a love for the whole of creation and beyond, pulsing and vibrating the eternal dynamic essence that you are.

9.   Now move to the forehead or brow chakra, seeing an indigo wheel of light three inches in diameter with a diamond, and spin the chakra on *HAY* three times. Your "all-seeing third eye" will open, and if you are of a disposition that allows intuition as an inspirational force to flood your being, you will perceive your angel and spirit guardians about you, loving you and watching over you. This is particularly beautiful within the context of opening to Metatron's force, which teaches through the metaphor of divine allegory.

10.   Penultimately, move to the crown chakra, three inches above the top of your head, and visualize a violet light within a beautiful diamond and sound *HEE* three times. Your aura will expand powerfully at this reckoning. Feel the waves of color vibration oscillating out from your physical membrane. This can be a deeply moving experience, so rest for a moment and soak in the textures of what you feel.

11.   We are now ready to move into the eighth chakra, which is located twelve inches above the violet hue of your crown chakra. This is the first transpersonal chakra, and connects us with the consciousness of the Universal Heart. When we associate our whole being with this chakra, waves of love move from us and to us for our brothers and sisters, for the whole of Mother Nature and Father Heaven, and the unseen forces that love our creation and serve its role in the creation of the cosmos. All these chakra sounds placed together are inspired to act as powerful sonic bells throughout the cosmos. The bells are invitations to those forces of the cosmos that correspond most with love. The angels, the

elementals, the unicorns, the ancient ones, and the Holy Spirit—meaning those beings that correspond wholeheartedly with the life-light circuitry. For, they are the agents of cosmic intelligence that help to align Planet Earth within the Divine Matrix.

12. Imagine a silver orb of light, seven inches in diameter, and as this chakra's nature is as an orb let it move in its own spherical directional. Sounding *HEE* three times, in a note that is coherent with this frequency, connects you to the current of its force. In human terms, the eighth chakra is the gateway to the dawning of Aquarius, so see the symbol for infinity placed above the spinning chakra.

13. Pause for a moment and imagine the whole of your energy field surrounded by a veil of golden light used to protect and shield your force. Then be still and receive the ministrations of love from all the beings in the cosmos that love you. In these moments we remember who we truly are. We remember that we are love untarnished, and we feel unmarked by the contaminations of the world, and free from the conceit of the ego. We sense ourselves to be soaking in a holy instant, where nothing matters other than what we be. For only when we move aside from the ego's account of us can we truly feel who we are, and what we are is whole, because we are holy. When we rest in this sacred moment we literally soak in the Source, remembering that, in fact, we never left; we simply fell asleep. Awakening from this River Lethe means we remember the Source and become "Sorcerers" again. We awaken to our true self, and this frees us from the nightmares of the material world. In this way, we become aligned with the mind of God. Our souls are extensions of this mind, the mind of God, and as such our truth is that we are divine. As we open our hearts completely to this power, both with God and the "we" of ourselves, our beings become the conduits for the miraculous.

14. Finally, as you see the golden light of protection all around you, notice how the sparkling hue of the gold insulates your causal body. See the white of your soul's sheath floating as a light body within the golden light of cosmic force. You will see this all around you, largely as a consequence of the golden light drawing the sanctity of the angelic kingdom toward you, and around you. Listen to the *sona*. You will possibly hear divine bells or voices; you may even bathe in the finer awareness of your own oracular presence.

15. Finally, **visualize yourself seated within a six-sided exquisitely cut diamond.** See the diamond as being twelve feet in height and six feet wide, for these proportions are wrought in the very breath of the divine. Rest for a moment in stillness and then say:

Dear Archangel Metatron:
Please touch me with your light and wrap me in your wings of protection.
Please wash my heart and soul clean of any impurities.
I venerate the exquisite quality of your elemental force, the sacred diamond,
and thank you for allowing me to be within its sanctuary.
Please allow the power of your teaching to penetrate deep into my heart
and soul, for the purpose of love and truth, for I adore the manna of your
presence.
Oh Holy One, bless me with your loving might and allow me to always be
your faithful servant.
So be it.
AMEN

End by drawing the light of Metatron's diamond deep into your cells, and sounding the heart vowel *AH*. This is the archangel of the covenant between human and divine. For it is written in the book of Exodus in the Bible: "Behold I send an Angel before thee, to keep thee in the way and to bring thee to a place that I have prepared."

After saying prayers or taking your meditation to another degree, simply sit in stillness and silence. Let the space of the silence pour into every cell of your body. Simply soak in the stillness. This is the core force of your life—this space is soul.

Then when you're ready, perhaps after ten or twenty minutes of stillness, close down each chakra by humming through the whole of your spine, seeing each light extinguish itself from top to bottom, before drawing in the pranic cord, and slowly, eventually moving from your sacred space. If you can, place a six-pointed amethyst crystal over your heart chakra, both front and back. This will protect you with divine force.

As you leave this space of your own reckoning, allow the diamond protecting your aura to reveal its presence in the world as your miraculous power of personal sovereignty. For this prism of a diamond is a microcosmic refraction of the divine.

Healing That Which Holds You in Darkness

Having experienced the healing force of sound caressing and nourishing you through the Diamond Sonic Meditation, you may have questions concerning "holding points" within your physical, emotional, or spiritual body.

I write of "holding points" rather than blockages because I believe that words anchor states within us, and that to receive healing we need to recognize the energy as objectively as possible. In this way, we remove the emotional drama related to the problem. This requires clarity, an avoidance of sentimentality, compassion concerning the issue that will be transmuted, and the willingness to quell negative emotion.

We will now use a classic diagnostic exercise from the Temple of Voice Alchemy. This particular process shines light into the darkness; it identifies the "holding" by naming it, so as to recognize its opposite value. This clarifies which chakra the "holding" is synthesized within. In turn, this indicates what color and sound can be used to help release and heal the holding. All energy is biodegradable if we allow it to let go and let God in. The work requires stillness, focus, discipline, and integrity.

Healing means a movement back to wholeness. *The Alchemy of Voice* suggests that working with sound is an effective ally for working with other complimentary disciplines. Sound as a vibration functions best as an agency for healing within the field of holistic wellness. This is particularly true when a disease state requires profound healing.

You will see that the following diagnostic process also includes the vibration of light and color with sound. Together, these energies harmonize the field of vibration. Remember, we are working with the core energies of Universal Force. The most powerful energy vibrating within the cosmos is that of light. The light from which all life springs exists in a threefold unity: the light of the sun, the light of spirit, and the light of thought. These three aspects of the one and only light form the ideas that lie behind the doctrine concerning the Holy Trinity.

Descending harmonies constellate the vast force of Earth's power matrix, which begins with light, downloads into color, then sound. It is the interaction of these forces with carbon, nitrogen, oxygen, hydrogen, and the three dimensions of weight, space, and time that brings together the constellation of harmonious forces that creates the extraordinary symphony we understand as Life.

Early Greek Mystery Schools took up the legacy of the earlier Atlantis and Egyptian Temples of Healing. These wisdom traditions taught that light "in-forms" and sound "trans-forms." Similarly, a maxim from the Orphic Mystery Schools of the sixth century B.C. suggests that light brings forth the ability to identify, whereas sound gives consciousness evidence of its existence. Interestingly, the word *orpheus* means "one who heals with light and sound." According to ancient stories, the Greek god Orpheus was gifted a beautiful lyre by Apollo. Using this lyre, he was able to make rocks and trees move and tame wild animals like Cerberus, who was becalmed by Orpheus's exquisite song. Enchantment was the key.

1. Find yourself a quiet place, taking pen and paper with you. If you have a friend to share this with you, even better. Light a candle, and release yourself from noise by moving into stillness and silence.
2. Breathe out and in on three occasions, then relax. Feel how responsive your whole cellular body is to the conviction of its own healing. Then ask yourself where you feel the "holding" in your body. If appropriate, discuss it with your partner.
3. If the pain or discomfort is located in a part of your physical body near a chakra, align with the energies of that chakra. (You will find specific identification of each chakra in Chapter 5)
4. If the pain is generalized, then ask yourself what color summarizes the discomfort. This information will lead you to the chakra associated with the lesion in your energy field.
5. However, if you choose a complimentary color, such as gray or brown or black, this means that:
   a. Other emotional energies surround the lesion;
   b. perhaps more than one chakra needs to be part of the healing process;
   c. or you are unclear about what you are feeling.
6. If the latter is the case, visualize the energy outside your body and in front of you, attached it to a cord light, then identify what colors you see and write them down.
7. Use the color lists in Chapter 5 to help you decipher the meanings associated with the colors. Decide what color is at the very locus of the lesion.
8. Determine which core word identifies the feeling. If necessary write the words down. When complete, distinguish which theme arises from the list. Choose one theme, otherwise your scrutiny will be confounded. Use your intuition and discuss it with your partner. What does this illuminate about the conviction of the feeling you experienced?

9. When you see the color, and feel the word, what age are you? A scenario may come to mind as a memory of something that took place, which created the holding. The list below will allow you to congruently perceive what created the lesion.

10. Discuss with your partner and then relate to the information below.

Chakra Evolution Chronology

RED – ROOT CHAKRA

This chakra awakens during the first eighteen months of life. It is associated with core identity issues—the way we relate to our ancestral patterns and gender or sexuality proclivities. As parental influence is obviously crucial, my commentary will concern the social norm of a two-parent family. When children are parented jointly, rather than existing in a one-parent situation, our psyche/soma energies reflect this nurturing. I am taking this approach for the sake of simplicity here, not from any position or prejudice.

During the first eighteen months of life, we are primarily aware of two people in our world. This is determined by sensory input and primary care needs: comforting, feeding, diapering, and bathing. One is Mother; generally farther away is Father. A very young child is still in contact with the inclusivity of the numinous, with the vast field of consciousness we know as Spirit. Differing parental energies can lead to isolation or confusion, displacing the flow of force and creating energetic deficits for the infant, as it seeks to get its needs met, and as it begins to develop as an earthling. This is highly significant and cannot be underestimated, so please take time to review the information noted in Chapter 5.

Ask yourself:
- What was your birth like?
- Were your parents absent or attentive?
- Were you born into an extended family, or one parent?
- Were there other siblings around to take care of you?
- Did your parents move home during this period?
- Were you well or unwell?
- Did you cry a lot, or were you peaceful?
- Was your mother able to suckle you?
- Do you carry ancestral patterns that result in karma?

Many questions may arise concerning this area of chakra development. Those listed above are designed to open thought landscapes and stimulate conversation between you and your dear partner. Many people remember little about their birthing and infant years, so talking to Mother, returning to the location of your early home, looking at photographs, speaking to grandparents or intimate relations, even visiting the hospital, clinic or location of your birthplace, can be exceptionally revealing. What were the sights, sounds, smells, tastes, and physical experiences of your first eighteen months of life?

Case Study

Emma came to me as a client experiencing sporadic physical bouts of dizziness and weight imbalance along with grave emotional challenges concerning her personal relationships. She had undergone all the usual allopathic diagnostic tools to investigate the physical symptoms, and nothing had been identified to determine the cause. Emma's father had died when she was sixteen years of age, while Emma was away at boarding school. Her mother didn't announce his death until two weeks after the interment, a fact that deeply angered Emma, even though, as she reported, her father had been absent most of her materially privileged life. She simply felt that her father was an extremely important aspect of her life, and that she should have been more lovingly informed.

Apart from the obvious and very unexpressed anger in relation to this, our conversation revealed that Emma had always felt deep love for her father, mixed with the shadow of resentment and loss. Emma felt displaced when her father had moved into high-status diplomatic service when she was born and her mother had veered between her own society commitments and Emma, who was chiefly brought up by three rather loving nannies. Emma's relationships with men were chaotic. She always sought out older men for intimacy, feeling protected by them, but their affections appeared to dwindle noticeably when she had opened herself to explore the sexual nature of their interaction.

It is often difficult to fully identify where the "holding" of energy lies within us, particularly as we rarely define specifically what we are feeling as we feel it. This is brought about by an imbalance in the right and left hemispheres of the brain, governing the ying and yang principles in the body. The left brain governs language and linear thought, while the right brain governs creativity and the world of emotion. Most people find it challenging to describe a feeling, subtle energy, or intuition, which requires a good connection between both hemispheres. It's a skill that comes with practice and worth developing. To imagine, visualize, or sense a sentient focus of energy outside our beings allows us a feeling of distance from subjective pain. It allows us to be objective through observation—the observer becomes the observed.

When I asked Emma to imagine the energy of what she was describing as a ball of force extending from her body, and to name it, she immediately uttered the word "betrayal." I then asked her what color she felt was associated with these feelings, and her answer was gray. Holding the grayness in her mind, I asked if she would describe the core of the gray, at which point she said yellow, red, and white—and that the white was a beautiful swirling light that held her in complete warmth and love!

Having interpreted the energetic holdings were located in the colors of red and yellow, I worked with the root chakra sound *HAW* and *HOH* for the solar plexus chakra, eventually drawing both energies into the eighth chakra of *HEE*, when I had intuited the energy had developed into a mass.

Emma was determined to concentrate her energies into transmuting the feelings of "betrayal" into "freedom" and from "anger" into "love." When she did this, she felt huge waves of healing moving through her. It was extraordinary witnessing huge amounts of subtle energy literally evaporating from her energy field.

INTENTION – FREQUENCY = HEALING

These three functions create a matrix of tremendous power, with which force may be transmuted. As we journeyed together through a series of sessions, we further identified the many problems and influences of her early years concerning the energetic holdings. Through using the principles of alchemy, Emma discovered a greater and greater ease. She is now living in a happy partnership with a man of her own age, and is the proud mother of a baby girl.

ORANGE – SACRAL CHAKRA

This chakra activates and evolves around two to three years of age and is associated with the behavior of primary relationship patterns. It relates to the dimensions of Weight, Space, and Time, as well as significant life experiences and relationships, including the early introduction to formal education (albeit mostly play-based) through kindergarten, nursery, or caretaker.

This period of growth is often described as the "terrible twos," illustrating the challenging behavior of the child experienced by Mother, Father, or Caregiver. I tender the opinion that this is the time when the young infant is made aware of both "doing" and "being." For example, "supermarket shouts" occur dramatically during this stage of development, when the child has simply had enough of "doing" and protests wildly "no more stimulation!"

If you were to place four two- to three-year-olds in a social context (a confined space such as a playpen) and encourage playful interaction, they would be interactive with one another up to a point, then when the mood shifts the children would literally stop "doing." and move into "being" mode, which is often constituted by turning their back on their peers. As the caretaker influence reappears and is negative in attitude to the behavior, turning the child around and encouraging activity, the child protests. As every parent knows, ire and frustration then pour forth.

Review the notion of relationship from a metaphoric and literal perspective, and reread the information about this chakra in Chapter 5.

Ask yourself:

- What were my primary relationships like at this time?
- Did I find motor action skills easy at this time?
- Where was my infant schooling (nursery) set?
- What was going on in the family at this stage?
- Did you have challenging or easy sibling interactions?
- Which parent did I interface with most?
- What sensory input did I enjoy at this time?
- Where certain activities or people favored?
- What clothes did I wear at this age?

Case Study

Ben came to me with acute prostatitis. This is a condition of the prostate gland causing groin pain, painful urination, and sexual problems. The prostate gland produces semen, the fluid that helps support and transport sperm. The gland is about the size of a walnut, sitting directly below the bladder and surrounding the urethra, the tube that transports both semen and urine through the penis.

Ben was a fifty-year-old executive with an extremely busy professional career and no significant personal relationship. Ben had suffered the pain and discomfort of the prostatitis for nearly a year and had been prescribed several anti-inflammatory drugs including antibiotics, in the belief that the condition was a bacterial infection. Ben had also received acupuncture, followed a macrobiotic food regime, and, other aspects of his life appeared on the surface to be healthy.

When I asked Ben to describe how he felt he replied "frustrated," yet smiled in response. I then asked him if he could tell me what his prostate felt, and he immediately said "abandoned" and looked very sad. I asked him what color he saw in his pained groin and he immediately cited dark purple.

Using the diagnostic tool of extending the energy from the body for objective rather than subjective exploration, I then asked what color he saw in the center of the purple and he replied dark orange. All my life I have seen force as color, then sound. I have learned to interpret this ability as synesthesia, a crossover of the senses. Whenever color appears dark in hue, my experience of reading aura always suggests that energy is severely depressed, leading to the possibility of disease.

When I asked Ben what had happened at the age of two or three, he responded that this was when he become aware of the intense unhappiness existing between his parents, strife-filled energies that had never been expressed. My intuition led me to believe that this lack of expressed energy was creating the purple force, and all the unexpressed abandonments, tears, anger, insinuations, pains, slights, hugs, dreams, loves, and hopes for change, fed the force. All of these and more were still held as energies. They were implicitly imprisoned but had also created the explicit and excessive "doing" in Ben's life, providing little room for just "being." This had become a feature of his life to the point where he could not develop intimate relationships, in case they led to scrutiny of those early years and what had unfolded ever since.

I used the sound *HOO* to work with the dark orange of the second chakra, and Ben concentrated on transmuting "Abandonment" into "Freedom." Ben's tears washed clean all the resentment of not being loved in the way that was so deeply desired. Release after release occurred, then fell silently into the vale of comfort that appears whenever we have expiated ourselves through deep mourning or renunciation.

I finished the process by drenching his aura in harmonic over-tones. These exquisite sounds alleviate the subtle forces that remain and allow a transcendental portal to open through Weight, Space, and Time to the celestial realms. The angels and spirit guardians are drawn through the loving intention in the sound to help with the cleansing work.

Ben and I worked thus on three further occasions over the next month, and his troubled pelvis gradually calmed and healed.

YELLOW – SOLAR PLEXUS CHAKRA

The development of this chakra begins around four to six years of age. It marks a time of crucial growth in the emotional center of the physical body, which is aptly associated with the *sol*, the sun.

The solar plexus holds a nerve center operating as a central locus for the production of "willpower," both the gain and loss of will. The glands closely associated with this area are the adrenal glands, situated on top of the kidneys in the region of the back below the ribs. The adrenals produce the chemical noradrenaline in connection with the "fight/flight" instinct of the sympathetic nervous system.

The development of self-realization around the substance of will arises between the ages of four and six. For example, take an incident such as little Freddie arriving home from an expedition to discover there is no movement in the hamster cage. On asking Mummy where Caspar the Hamster is, Mummy replies: "He's gone to sleep forever!" Now most young children appear to have little difficulty with this information, be-cause so much of their world is in connection with the numinous, through unseen guides or imaginary companions. But, on this occasion Freddie notices the tears falling from Mummy's eyes and is immediately disturbed. Up to this point, the child's experience of life had been set for perpetuity, and now it is redefined as a result of the feeling of loss created by Mother's weeping. Within this situation, she has an opportunity to introduce rather radical information about Life and Death. The question is: will she take that opportunity?

My experience of thousands of clients over the years would suggest that many mothers weren't able to produce the information required at such a time, so weighty ancestral dilemmas are handed to the child concerning a loss and gain of will. For more on this, read the statement concerning the naval chakra in Chapter 5.

Ask yourself:
- Do you feel your ego is easy with the use of will?
- Are you someone who has lots of willpower?
- When was it that you last felt a loss of will?
- Can you remember what it felt like to gain will?
- Who has a tenacious will among those you know?
- How many people do you know who give up easily?
- The main thing is to keep the main thing, the main thing. Can you?
- List those life situations you know most create loss?
- Where do you mostly feel gain/loss in your body?

Case Study

Jennifer was sixteen years old when her parents asked me to work with her. Jennifer's mother was a client of mine and an avid supporter of *The Alchemy of Voice*.

Jennifer experienced great difficulty sitting examinations, even though she possessed an extrovert, highly likable personality and was intelligent and industrious in her studies. For her, something indefinable occurred each time she approached the idea of being tested. Nervousness consumed her; furthermore, these feelings made her feel dizzy and nauseous. I asked her if she could identify any other time in her life when similar feelings had arisen. All she could recount was a similar sensation occurring when she started secondary school, and then before the first couple of dates with her boyfriend Julian, whom she had been happily dating for nearly a year. Although they were young, the relationship between these two young people seemed full of balance in the way they supported each other through school (different schools), and the burgeoning life lessons they experienced.

I asked Jennifer if any other parts of her body felt affected by the discomfort or pain, and she reported that her upper waist on the left side of her body through the pelvic area often felt very tender. As she placed her hand on this area of her body, her hand rested on the general kidney area, just where the adrenal gland lies. Interestingly, these symptoms only occurred during "testing" situations.

Using the diagnostic tool that is the bedrock of Voice Alchemy, I asked Jennifer to visualize the pain as a ball of energy moving in front of her and to visualize it as a color. She immediately reported "dark brown." We ventured farther to its center, at which point Jennifer suggested she saw clearly dark yellow.

Brown is an energy indicating process, or life in transition; often, when very dark, the energy represents stagnation. However, as we all may observe in nature, the bright flora of summer diminishes in autumn, becomes brown, falls to the earth, and then life is created anew in spring.

I encouraged Jennifer to see this as an allegory of what she was experiencing during this important time of her life. Examinations were her immediate preoccupation, and an indication of "life in transition." I enquired what had happened in her life during the time between the fourth and sixth year, around her fifth year, and Jennifer spoke of her highly successful father losing his executive position at a multinational company through being made redundant. This job loss had produced hardship in the family, and Jennifer had unconsciously absorbed much of the family's stress into her third chakra. She could remember copious rows taking place between her mother and father, and how she often felt terribly divided between them, even though their post-row mollification of each another was visible within family life. It was obvious that they both cared deeply about one another and were sorely tested at this time.

Jennifer's fear of exams, whether this be success or failure, was brought about by the fear she experienced in her father, observed at five years of age. Father and daughter were extremely close, and often synergistically experienced similar ailments, such as stomach upsets and indigestion. They both felt challenged by patriarchy, and tests produced fear because it made them both feel vulnerable and susceptible to harsh criticism. My experience suggests that this is a common phenomenon in the competitive nature of the patriarchal context, when the shadow aspect of human consciousness is denied. Often there is a great fear of individual success within a person because of the evident responsibility that arrives with it. Does success create approbation or disapprobation in your life?

We worked for some time on the sound HOW around Jennifer's third chakra, transmuting "Fear" into "Joy," and continued this work through three or four further sessions. This gave us time to also embrace an intuitive diagnosis and self-empowerment processes. By aligning intention with sound and exploring the precise frequency we radically alleviated Jennifer's fear of success. Soon, her feeling of being judged in testing situations was a thing of the past.

GREEN – HEART CHAKRA

The heart chakra stimulates growth and awareness that lead to self-knowledge between the ages of seven and nine years of age. This is the period when we develop a level of consciousness that reflects the substance of both conditional and unconditional love, even though its overt behavior may not arise until a later period in life.

Self-distinction is a common theme at this time of maturation. The seven- to nine-year-old child is beginning to develop specific choices about life, even if these appear self-concentric, such as: "I want to wear the blue socks not the red socks," or "I want to eat fish fingers not spaghetti." If negotiations with the child are handled well at this stage, by emotionally intelligent and understanding parents, the capacity for self-belief grows. Initially, this may appear self-oriented; later in life, however, as greater experience develops, the individual will be able to make personal decisions very easily.

Ask yourself:
- How powerful is your love?
- Where do you feel love most in your body?
- Are you conditional or unconditional in your loving?
- When did you first "fall in love?"
- Does loving make you feel powerless?
- List words that you associate with conditional and unconditional love
- Is it difficult to make decisions?
- Can you organize yourself effectively?
- How successful are your negotiating skills?

Case Study

Xavier, an American citizen, became a client of mine while I served a theater project in the United States a few years ago. The company manager, Xavier disclosed to me that he found great difficulty making primary decisions about any personal matter: whether to date this person or that person, what to wear, what to eat, where to live, what to buy as a gift for someone dear, or what to do in any emotionally charged intimate situation. Yet when dealing with any professional exigency or situation, he was a highly thoughtful caregiver and a first-rate manager; nothing was too much for him to achieve; his intuitive management style and his social diplomacy skills were first class. Xavier is one of the few people I've met who is able to disagree without being disagreeable.

However, the level of disparity between his personal and professional life was marked, and this behavior left him feeling disassociated and often depressed. Xavier asked me for a consultation, which I gladly gave.

Once again, I asked the diagnostic questions:
a. Where do you feel the "holding" in your body?
b. What color is it when externalized from your physique?
c. What is the energy of the "holding" called?
d. How young or how old does the negativity make you feel?
e. What will it feel like with the transmutation complete?

The answers that came were:
a. Xavier placed his hand on his heart.
b. Xavier saw a ball of dark blue/black, then green, then bright white light.
c. Xavier felt the energy was called "Fear" and "Loss."
d. Xavier said he felt eight or nine years of age.
e. Xavier's face immediately lit up when he said: "Freedom, full of love."

Xavier's responses came naturally, before I could outline why I was asking the questions. Xavier said he felt a passionate trust, and the easy flow gave confirmation about how instinctive his observations were; there was literally no hesitation.

Our subtle body is a powerhouse of unique energy, galvanized by our chakras spinning light into our energy field. The aura is motivated by the will, our instinct to create physical life from mental intention, and the condition of our emotional body. It is the combination of our software (energy field) and hardware (DNA) that brings about change. Through will, clear intention, and frequency we may transmute energy, altering patterns of behavior that are often many years old, or indeed linked with karma or ancestral patterns.

I asked what had happened in his eighth year of life, and immediately Xavier spoke of his father's death at that time. The responsibility he then felt to take care of his mother and younger sister arrested his own innate process.

When our emotions are dramatically held back from expression in life, often as a result of trauma, we mostly describe the quality of the force as black or dark blue. Of course, black indicates a lack or absence of color and can be associated with force that is sinister and negative in form, or potential energy that is inchoate, as it is when we peer into the "void" of our own psyche. In Xavier's case, this concerned the terrible news of his father's heart attack, and how he immediately held inside the emotional force that came with it of fear, terror, loss, abandonment, and anger. He held back so that he could cope with his mother's profound loss and his younger sister's tears. In the face of such anguish, it is not surprising that profound indecision could become a personal characteristic.

The heart chakra is the locus and seat of the soul. Its flow leads us to an expression of joy about our whole life. Conversely, if energies are withheld, we are personally compromised in making any decision that may affect life. For example, in extreme situations in our lives, when everything suddenly changes, what would happen if we made the wrong decision? What would happen if no decision was made? What would happen if a decision leads to freedom? Is there approbation (personal or other) granted for the wonderment that has been achieved?

All of this and more became the common ground on which Xavier and I worked through the trauma of that intense period in his eight-year-old life. In many ways, the ground we trod through in those moments together presented new paradigms for Xavier's future life. As I sounded *HA* through his chest, first by intending the loss that his inner child had experienced, and then by living the joy of freedom in love from my own heart, Xavier's held force exploded in his chest and he wept long and bitter tears. I held him in my arms until much of the force had been expressed.

The poignancy of sound as a healing modality moves us to the very nexus of our truth. Often, by administering sound, many years of denial can be expressed and released. Often, when people have observed this quality of healing taking place in workshop situations, they speak of how palpable, how swift, and how vast the healing appears to be.

BLUE – THROAT CHAKRA

The throat is a conduit between the liberating sensations of the body and the myriad thoughts of the head, and as such has always been known as a mystical corridor of life. Just attempt chanting *AUM* on thirty-three breaths in your meditation practice at sunrise and sundown, and notice the extraordinary difference to your body/mind power. The throat is a sonic viaduct for the divine nature of communication. As such, it is a link to the potential fulfillment of a sacred act: your self-expression. It is a bridge between the purely abstract nature of cosmic life and the relativity of Earth-borne existence. Self-expression and communication are its seed mantras; blue is its color.

The Sanskrit name for this chakra is *Vishuddhi*, meaning "to purify," and so through the energy of this chakra our lower energies are uplifted into the purification of the sacred, which is the source from which sound first arose.

The throat chakra's constitution leads us to the ability whereby we discriminate between comprehension and realization. Through it we discern the information percolating from the physical experience of life, with all its bubbling unconscious chatter and the higher levels of wisdom received like divine nectar. The Word of the Logos brings with it spiritual nourishment that refines the experience of life, and therefore, this energy center represents a gateway of openness that perceives all experience as a teaching, leading to profound understanding.

When the throat chakra is open, the unconditional love of the heart finds its means to expression, and so truth is spoken. Many of our leading wisdom cultures refer to the throat chakra as the physical entry-exit point of the soul. In my experience of working with the dying, I have seen "soul force" leaving the physical body of the person at the point of his or her death, breathed out through the throat and mouth, returning to the field of light that is eternal.

In life, the throat chakra begins to awaken around the age of ten to thirteen years old, although this chronology is entirely dependent on the individual's maturation process. The thyroid gland wraps around the larynx, from which the note arises, and secretes hormones that help to regulate metabolism, particularly active during adolescence.

Ask yourself:
- Do I like my voice and how self-expressive is it?
- Do I enjoy communication?
- Is life rich with joyous talk, or is it challenging to speak or sing?
- Do I talk too much, or do I talk too little?
- Are my words filled with discernment or higher choice and wisdom?
- Do I wish to improve my voice?
- Do I use speaking to create a wall of sound as protection or defence?

- Am I frightened of speaking in public?
- Where does my voice come from in my body?

Case Study

Anita came to me as an executive who was making a significant contribution to the world, specifically as the CEO of a successful pan-global company. Anita was a highly experienced public speaker/presenter, required to speak formally in many situations, such as addressing board meetings, company strategy meetings, annual general conferences, and public and business forums, when she would often speak to hundreds or thousands of people.

Anita was an activist truth seeker—the very embodiment of a warrior goddess. She felt deep concern about all issues to do with social justice, democratic fairness, social reformation through emotional intelligence, eco-sustainability, and human capital abundance. The fervency with which she held her beliefs had led to her being actively involved in several major charities.

Athough she was a powerful speaker, Anita lacked heartfelt passion and the kind of inspiration that comes from the soul. Her style was brow-beating and aggressive, and we both agreed that the ingredients of gentleness and compassion would be important to acquire and become part of her style of delivery. In effect, she needed to balance the warrior qualities of Pallas Athena with the loving qualities of Aphrodite.

My experience of major personalities in the fields of world media and corporate communication—I've coached a number of states-people and politicians—is that they rarely have time for coaching. They often avoid the issue of bettering their performance, feeling sensitive about being placed under the microscope of the training. Frequently in these situations behavioral reactions trigger the ego, so it takes a secure personality to step forward and request help.

Many people are fearful of public speaking. For example, international statistics suggest that more people would prefer to be in the coffin than making the speech at the funeral. I have specialized in this particular area of voice work for many years. My years of experience have shown that working with the Alchemy of Voice can help dispel fear from people's hearts and encourage them toward a sense of personal empowerment. After all, happiness is a decision not a condition.

Anita's first consultation was primarily diagnostic, a way for us to get to know one another. On the second consultation, after she began to feel more relaxed, she shared with me that whenever she became nervous about public speaking, she felt a huge lump appear in her throat. On one occasion the feeling had been so intense and long-lasting, she had consulted a laryngologist. He had found nothing untoward, however.

In order to shed light on the meaning of this lump in Anita's throat and reassure her that it was not cancerous, I opened up the conversation to include a discussion of voice physiology. Pioneering psychologist Carl Jung referred to the throat as "a ring of fear" because the sphincter muscles in the trachea close whenever we are afraid. This leads to the impression that our throat or windpipe has a large obstruction in it.

I then used the diagnostic tool related to the throat chakra so that we could investigate this phenomenon further:

- What color does the lump feel like, when externalized from your body?
- Do you feel the lump anywhere else in your physique?
- What would you call the lump?
- How young does it make you feel?

Anita responded without hesitation, saying:

- I see dark blue with flecks of light blue in the center.
- Yes, in my heart.
- Regret. Loss. Frustration.
- I feel about twelve years of age.

This opened up the subtle dimension of the feeling-body and allowed us to explore deeper the meaning of what was going on. Anita disclosed that she had been truly torn apart by her parents' divorce during her twelfth year, which constituted moving home and location. Being an only child, she and her mother moved from a very comfortable home and privileged, salubrious lifestyle to a home and lifestyle of more modest means. The change in schools necessitated by the move had its own effect. Always an outstanding student with high grades, Anita became a middle-of-the-road student with low grades. Her memory of that time was that she became shy, fractious, and of a nervous disposition.

Our work together involved transmuting the sadness that accompanied the negative feelings of regret and loss she had felt at her parents' divorce into feelings of positive acceptance and gain. Now Anita began to see that, in fact, her parents divorce had opened the road to new ways of being, new projects, and new friends. Her adolescent experiences had both light and dark shades to them—experiences that allowed her to develop a strength of character that led her to university and her later occupational successes. Anita could now acknowledge her own considerable ability to create abundance from adversity. She recognized now that thought creates reality—as Einstein said: what we visualize we materialize.

In the vocal work, we focused on opening Anita's throat chakra, using the sound of *HI* while concentrating on the color light blue and working to shift the thought forms that arose, from negative to positive.

We began by entraining the feeling connected with "Loss," and to thereby transmute it into the "Joy of Gain." At this point, the combined use of breath, intention, sound frequency, and resonance brought about a profound shift in Anita. She felt a tremendous freedom opening in her neck and a weight lifting from her chest. Her heart chakra opened to heal the lack of forgiveness she had held in her heart as a result of her parents' divorce. This was a huge realization which healed the wide gulf between Anita and her parents that had existed for many years and allowed her to let go of the blame she had felt at the thought that they had "ruined" their lives.

Our final work was to plan Anita's presentations, employing the notion of the second Sonic Chamber of "I soothe" and the third chamber "I empower" (For more on this, see Chapter 4 of *The Alchemy of Voice* and my CD "Awakening"). This allowed Anita to develop a smoother, richer, more weightier tone. The tone now was less cerebral, less strident, and more suited for the new energy of balancing the Goddess of War with the Goddess of Love. It allowed a Sorceress to step forward—vibrant, sexy, magical, and mesmerizing.

Anita now felt that her attitude toward social injustice was balanced with a spiritual temperance that naturally arose from her understanding the significance of cause and effect. Our work also clarified for Anita the nature of the conviction that lay beneath her pioneering work, which she said was suffused by the energy of the color turquoise. She eventually relinquished her position as CEO, became a magistrate, and moved deeper into her life work: bringing justice to the underprivileged, all over the world.

INDIGO – BROW CHAKRA

The brow chakra develops between the ages of fourteen and seventeen years of age. It is the chakra of the mind, or objectivity. At this time in an adolescent's high school career, they make decisions about which future examinations they will be taking and the nature of the work to be done to achieve those ends. This requires discernment, which develops at this stage of life. The common trait associated with this time in a healthy adolescent is heightened self-awareness, combined with an inherent joy, inner vision, and certitude. But of course, the shadow is also lurking, too, leading to the opposite emotional values being displayed in an adolescent.

In many of our world's spiritual traditions, the brow chakra is known as the vestigial "third eye," or "the eye of wisdom." It focuses our imagination, inner seeing, and intuition, opening us to the possibility of psychic or oracular visioning. Inevitably, inner seeing leads us to transcendent wisdoms, and in fact, the Sanskrit name for this chakra is *ajna*, meaning "to command"—that through transcendent knowing we may transform base yearnings into inner truth and wisdom. The connection between this chakra and the crown center above enables higher knowledge to be available to the individual.

As our "third eye" wakes up, we develop the ability to see things clearly using intuitive knowledge. We are awake to the power of cause and effect, to the fact that everything is interdependent, and that we can truly perceive the subtle energy that governs the law of manifestation in our world and the cosmos.

Ask yourself:
- Do I concentrate my energies into objectivity?
- Am I lost in an ocean of feeling and sentimentality?
- Do I practice developing my in-tuition?
- Am I balancing my heart and my knowledge with effect?
- Do I have spiritual faith?
- Do I blame and accuse, or am I full of insight and resolution?
- How powerful is my imagination?
- Am I engaging in charitable acts for the whole of nature?
- What am I doing to produce spiritual wealth on Planet Earth?

THE ALCHEMY OF VOICE

Matthew was an ex-student of mine and had become a very successful film actor. Matthew was debonair, charming, had classic good
looks, stylish demeanor, and a vocal sensuality that brought raptures
to his audience. As his confidence, grew he became more and more
creatively explosive and risk-taking in the roles that he played, and
consequently had been chosen by leading movie-makers to play leading roles.

Everything in Matthew's life appeared excellent. He had married
his partner of several years, and recently they had had their first child,
who was a beautiful addition to the wonderment of his life. However,
something deep within Matthew's psyche would frequently creep to
the surface of his consciousness, bringing with it a feeling of depression and worthlessness. He sought me out.

We ventured into the diagnostic procedure I have described
before:

- What color is the feeling when you see it as an external force?
- Where do you feel it in your physique?
- What is the feeling called?
- Do you feel you can be objective in trying situations?
- How young does it make you feel?
- What happened at that stage of your life?

Matthew responded:
- Black, dark blue, gray, and purple or indigo.
- Its like a headache, but then spreads.
- Depression. Or confusion and guilt.
- No, I seem to lose the thread, and an autopilot takes over.
- About sixteen.
- I met my first serious lover.

Further conversation revealed the story of how Matthew had fallen in
love with a congregation member of the parish church he attended every Sunday as a child. Matthew's parents were devout Christians living
in the leafy suburbs of a North American city, who practiced their belief
through charitable acts of unconditional love within their community.
They truly were beneficent people, and loved their son deeply.

However, the object of Matthew's affection was Rupert, the son of
the parish priest, and when knowledge of their liaison become public,

his lover was rejected by his own mother and father and sent away from the community, "to cure him of his infatuation."

Matthew had felt deeply angry and resentful at this decision, and as he had no way of accessing Rupert—who had moved many miles away—he stopped attending Holy Communion in protest. This action effectively switched off his connection with what had been a devoted path, with Jesus at the zenith. Matthew saw prayer as a central part of his faith; he felt it to be vital, not as a refuge but as a reverence. To close off this flow with Source, with all that he considered pure and good, was traumatizing.

Matthew didn't see Rupert again for many years, by which time he had sexually matured. He professed himself to be bisexual, a fact that was completely understood by his wife, whom he felt completely faithful to, hence, their marriage. Meeting Rupert again after so many years caused the energy stifled by remorse to once more emerge from deep in his unconscious, even though Matthew no longer felt deep love for Rupert. Time and experience change us; we mature and evolve, developing other tastes and predilections. This doesn't necessarily indicate that we are superficial, but rather that we are responding to life's creative flow, where we may love and live deeply without feeling the need to connect with the object of our affection, as we did when much younger. This is if we can emotionally mature.

What Matthew had effectively achieved was to suppress the force of his *ajna* chakra, his link with the inspirational flow of the divine. Of course, these energies had been converted into other forces needed to support his artistic work as an actor; however, because the expressions of Matthew's belief, faith, and trust in a higher power were stifled, emotions such as depression had arisen instead.

The diagnostic process had given us all the answers we needed. The black, dark blue, and gray colors Matthew saw were a representation of the void in which he had held himself. They represented the bruised condition of his psyche from resentment, anger, and guilt, and emotional confusion regarding homosexual feelings that had not been allowed full expression.

We worked on the transmutation of feeling in the following way:

RESENTMENT – DETACHMENT
ANGER – LOVE
GUILT – INNOCENCE
DEPRESSION – EXPRESSION

I used the vowel sound *HAY* moving into *EE* to purify Matthew's brow chakra, then sculpted the sound into harmonic overtones, which purified further the density of the held upper energies. Matthew began to weep tears of unexpressed anger that had been held back for sixteen or seventeen years. This was a highly refined attuned healing, and Matthew has now returned to the devotion of his spiritual path, resolved within a Tibetan Buddhist practice. The joy he felt reconnected him with charitable deeds, and when he last communicated with me he was researching the possibility of becoming a spiritual counselor.

VIOLET – CROWN CHAKRA

Most of our chakras exist within the realm of the human psyche, but with the crown and the esoteric eighth, ninth, tenth, eleventh, and twelfth chakras we travel through transpersonal energies and move into the celestial aspect of the human energy field, and beyond into the Universal Field itself. The chakras beyond the eighth are reactivating at this time of extraordinary spiritual development, and I will be dealing with these esoteric chakras in future writings illuminating the evolution of *The Alchemy of Voice*.

The crown chakra is connected to the pineal gland, which is known as the "seat of the soul." It is the gateway to pure spiritual intelligence, a vector to the oneness that exists when connection is made with what is variously referred to as the Divine, God Consciousness, or Communion with the Infinite. At that point, all duality vanishes, and All Becomes One.

The crown chakra develops between the ages of eighteen and twenty-one years of age. This can only occur if there is sufficient awareness for, as we know, many of our brothers and sisters believe that it is inappropriate to connect with a spiritual path, so their crown chakra lies dormant.

A spiritual journey involves a movement back to wholeness. We move toward enlightenment through humble, heartfelt practice. When we reach the sacred destination of this chakra, we radiate compassion, empathy, love, and the highest choice ever.

Ask yourself:
- Do I have connection with the spiritual nature of my being?
- Am I resourcing all my life choices from the core of my love?
- Am I interested in drawing the light of supreme intelligence into my physical and emotional body?
- Would I be interested in a pathway to enlightenment?
- Do I see that the whole of life exists connectively?

- What spiritual teachings do I wish to connect with?
- Do I feel that charity is a noble action?
- How can spirituality lead to a path of truth, when the world says other?
- Do I believe in nonduality?

Case Study

Hilary approached me at a Mind, Body & Spirit Congress to request assistance. She was very unwell; the simple truth was that Hilary had six months to live, as her body had been diagnosed with cancer. It was time for Hilary to pass from physical life into eternity, and the question on her lips was how could this occur as lovingly, as painlessly, as comfortably, and as nobly as possible.

During our conversation, Hilary announced that she had no faith in religion, God, the Afterlife, or the Eternal; she felt these were all false constructs and that her body would simply decay. I asked her if she believed in love, joy, peace, hope, truth, and beauty as a means to change, to grow. For me to assist her, Hilary would have to believe in her ability to discern, value, and honor the richness and meaning of life and all its mysteries, to transcend the mundane by aspiring for excellence and wishing to seek a broader intelligence that is our birthright.

Hilary acceded and agreed that she felt these virtues were fair and just, and we began bi-weekly treatments, during which I surrounded her with incandescent sound. During our sessions there was always so much pink and golden light around Hilary, and we were able to transmute much of the fear that had created the cancer, located in her second and third chakras. The pink signified her soul's connection with the divine; the gold was a gift from the angelic kingdoms. All was suffused with such pure love.

Because I believe that prayer helps us transcend our troubles, I frequently asked if I could read and repeat one of my favorite prayers. It was created by a Roman Catholic deacon in the twelfth century in Italy who became known as St. Francis of Assisi. Prayer is an important element of the life of spirit, for as we intercede we open powerful vectors that interweave with the purest energy within the cosmos, the love-light circuitry. It is the intention of prayer that allows us to speak to God. This is distinct from meditation, which allows us to listen to the Eternal All That Is.

Prayer of St. Francis

"Lord make me an instrument of thy peace.
Where there is hatred, let me sow love,
Where there is injury, pardon,
Where there is doubt, faith,
Where there is despair, hope,
Where there is darkness, light,
Where there is sadness, joy.

O Divine Master, grant that I may not so much seek
To be consoled as to console,
To be understood as to understand,
To be loved as to love:
For it is in giving that we receive,
It is in pardoning that we are pardoned,
It is in dying that we are born to eternal life."

Hilary and I often wept together as we savored these words. She kept the prayer with her throughout the remaining journey of her life. Those moments of sharing were some of the deepest experiences I've had with another human being. The more we contemplated the holy compassion within St. Francis's words, the more intense our joy became, forming a spectacular and vast connection with the divine. Each time we repeated the words, the sonic transmission carried something from the stillness and silence of the cosmos deep into our cells.

Our shared love and passion for life expressed itself through many conversations—not just philosophic and worldly but humorous, too. All was true, all sublime, and we met in silver light just before her time of passing. We dedicated our lives to the Great Light—a light that I saw pulsing from God to all of humanity, in order to heal, inspire, salve, and inspire. I had a deep knowing during those moments that this invisible and yet visible light is there to offer succor to all.

Just before Hilary's death, I often used the sacred harmonics that the angels have given me. These divine songs focused the electrical frequency of the silver soul using the crown chakra tone of *HEE*, then the sound sculpted into incandescent shimmerings of light. Hilary was very funny, as she told me that these sounds calmed her with a magical bliss better than any orgasm, which made us both laugh hysterically. Although I wasn't with her when she died, I was aware that Hilary's crown chakra had become a pulsating luminescent light violet throughout her remaining time.

Sounding the Sacred Om

Chanting, or sounding, the *OM* is one of the most elevating and joyous ways of raising one's frequency to become more receptive. It allows us to open pathways of intelligence that supersede the mundane, and to heal the pressures that we may develop as we journey through these remarkable shifting points of time.

> *"The OM is the essence of essence, the highest.*
> *Venerated above all that human beings hold holy,*
> *OM is the self of all, for with OM we say "I agree"*
> *And with OM we fulfill desire.*
> *With OM, we recite and give direction,*
> *We sing aloud the honor of the Word,*
> *Which is the key to knowledge."*
> —*CHANDOGYA UPANISHAD*

When we sound the *OM*, or *AUM*, we chant the most sacred seed syllable of all syllables. This is the *logos*, the essence of the Source, made intelligible by the Word, reflecting "the word that was made flesh and dwelt in grace and truth."

The *AUM* is divine consciousness made manifest here on Earth. So imagine that when you sound the *AUM*, you are part of the evolving cosmic consciousness. This is the sound with which the whole of creation resonates; therefore, it is the sound that began the reverberation of creation through God's own voice.

1. Sit in your sacred space, or in a power spot. Switch on voicemail or otherwise make sure you will not be disturbed.
2. Burn a candle and some incense to purify and elevate the consciousness of the space and your energy field.
3. Sit quietly for a moment feeling the rhythm of your breath, slow and full, noticing Silence, Stillness, and Solitude.
4. Make sure your spine is aligned and that you feel gravity in your body. Use the *mudra* that brings an even greater concentration to the whole of your body.

5. Begin to expand the breath by opening the rib cage, and when you feel the breath has warmed gently intone a *HUM* note through your heart chakra. Repeat this three times, checking that it is comfortable and without tension and that you are sitting in your signature note—the song of your soul.

6. Gradually, open the breath further and sound *AH – AW – OO – MM (AUM* or *OM)*, as though you are sculpting it through the whole of your mouth or palate.

7. Do this 77 times, feeling the sacred sound resonating in your pelvis, chest, and head.

8. Finish by once more sitting in Silence, Stillness, and Silence, simply being aware of the incandescent splendor of that peace and joy you connect with deep in yourself, and in the cosmos. Soaking in the stillness of soul is one of the many instruments of the Temple of Works known as *The Alchemy of Voice*. May it bring you peace, love, and healing.

AMEN.

THE HEART'S NOTE

Sounding Love in Your Life
from Your Heart's Secret Chamber

THE HEART'S NOTE shares powerful insights into the knowledge of the heart as the seat of the soul, and how a practical daily application of loving can create answers to the myriad problems we find ourselves facing at this time of vast planetary change, whether this be as a result of economic hardship, climate change, our relationships, our health or our career. The intention of the book is to take us back to the heart, that fundamental aspect of our physiology where we may rediscover the true inner peace with which we were born.

The book shows us how we may experience harmony and love, with which we may make our lives more peaceful and fulfilling. The information shared is garnered from the direct experience of Stewart Pearce as a scholar and teacher, who has pioneered Sound Healing for over twenty years as well as Voice Coaching household names, and provides the reader with an opportunity to experience the inspirational, uplifting and empowering teaching models that characterize his personal appearances.

Stewart reveals with purity and precision that love is not a mere sentiment, but the ultimate truth at the heart of creation.

ISBN 978-1-84409-506-3

FINDHORN PRESS

Life Changing Books

For a complete catalogue,
please contact:

Findhorn Press Ltd
117-121 High Street,
Forres IV36 1AB,
Scotland, UK

t +44 (0)1309 690582
f +44 (0)131 777 2711
e info@findhornpress.com

or consult our catalogue online
(with secure order facility) on
www.findhornpress.com

For information on the Findhorn Foundation:
www.findhorn.org